T0022814

Cordite
&
Testosterone

***why men should
not be running the world

by
Cecilia Tanner

Trafford rev. 01/27/2012

 www.trafford.com

North America & international
toll-free: 1 888 232 4444 (USA & Canada)
phone: 250 383 6864 ✦ fax: 812 355 4082

Contents

This book is dedicated
to everyone's children

(1) MEN CAN'T BE TRUSTED TO RUN THE WORLD

March 2008 headlines:
Prince Harry Goes to War.
In February 2008, Prince Harry of England went to "the front lines" in Afghanistan for 10 weeks.

Why?

Because he wanted "to be one of the lads." How many men or near-men want to kill and be killed "to be one of the lads"—not even to rescue democracy which is also fatuous altruistic nonsense, ie. killing people to save their lives? or restoring a democracy that never existed? But the press gleefully and admiringly reported how wonderful it was that Prince Harry just wanted "to be one of the lads".

And he went to the "front lines". They find this even more admirable since they love the old war talk. But where are the front lines in Afghanistan? They don't line up and charge with bayonets on the rifles anymore. Did someone draw a line in the dirt for Prince Harry?

This is just too much; words absolutely fail me. Did we ever see Queen Elizabeth take up a gun and stride to the *frontlines* "to be one of the lasses"?

Prince Harry's older brother, Prince William, has expressed sorrow that he wasn't able to go to the front like his younger brother.
The fundamental argument in this book is that males have different drives than females, and the activities they undertake to gratify those drives are destroying the human race *and* the planet.

Running the world is one activity that should be gender neutral because males and females have an equal stake in the outcomes of local, national and international decisions. There is no evidence in the whole world that indicates male leadership is good for the world, because when you mix testosterone & cordite, common sense, reason, and sanity disappear.

Feminists claim women do feminine things because they have been socialized to do so. Women do female things because they are women. Men and women are not better or worse than each other, just different. The Yin is not better than the Yang. What women *have been* socialized to accept is male supremacy. The author Barbara Kingsolver remarked, "At some time in their lives, girls look around to see who is running the world, and it's not women," and they don't know why.

Women all over the world have been conditioned to defer to men in "important matters". Look at every summit meeting—all males— maybe one woman. Look at the propaganda leading up to every trumped up war; suddenly women disappear and we see the heroics of male decision-makers "stepping up to the plate" to defeat evil and keep the world safe for their women and children. There is no room for the voice of women. War means that it will be necessary to slaughter the mother's children in many hideous ways, so their silence is essential.

Cordite and Testosterone expands on the specific evidence of the male as an unworthy leader, looking at some male phenomenon such as male competition. One example is the male need to achieve the biggest, the tallest, the best, the most, whether it be the most money, the tallest building, the fastest car or the most luxurious yacht.

When men enter into the big competitions, they do so under honorable motives or at least purport to espouse such good motives. But when the competition gets underway, the greed and the power abuse take over. In Iran, the Islamic promise after the downfall of the Shaw, Reza Pahlavi, in 1979, was to create a fair and just Islamic society. And what did they get when the dust settled? Terrorization of the whole country and brutal oppression of the women. Women were forced to hide because they might excite the men sexually, which was ruled to be criminal. The vice squads patrolling on motorcycles and trucks would arrest women (mostly young) who revealed too much sock, or skin around their scarves, or talked to any man not their guardian, and then the vice squads tortured the women, flogged them, and jailed them where the women were "searched" and often raped, if not killed or both. This was not a crime in Iran. This they did in the pursuit of a better society.

Then Ayatollah Komeini vowed to kill all the infidels—this when he was fighting the war with Iraq, a Muslim country. When not fighting the Muslim *infidels* of Iraq, he vowed death to all Americans—the other infidels. Clearly, a very confused man. The whole country of Iran under Ayatollah Komeini was bedlam. Power turned into utter madness.

The whole world is male oriented, and human society is sick as a result.

Because patriarchy is in the interests of men, they will never willingly relinquish their advantages. Women have tried to make the changes. Women in the early 20th Century wanted the right to vote, the right to own property, the right to choose pregnancy, the right to better paying jobs. It was a drive for equal rights. We got some—some of us got some.

(In 2007, President Sarkozy chose to appoint almost as many women to his cabinet in France as men appointees. This was hopeful until we find that Sarkozy surrounded himself by many corrupt men who have the same old greed factor in their decisions.)

Now women have to go beyond that. Men can't seem to discipline themselves to put the most important priorities at the top of their Do lists so women have to write the Do lists and make sure the men do those obligations first, then play their games. Nothing less.

Since the ill-taken invasion of Afghanistan, many men all over the world have taken on the fight mode and are looking for trouble. When I saw the stats of the murdered Iraqis and Americans in the Iraq war, 100,000 Iraqis and 4500 Americans—not even mentioning the dead British allies or other civilians—I was reminded of the image of the man who started the Iraq War being interviewed on a golf course during the war who commented when he thought he was off camera, "Okay, take a look at this swing,"—while people were being slaughtered. Even Attila the Hun was more engaged in his brutality than that.

Are we going to ignore the signs of this potential Armageddon hoping it will just go away? No one stops them because men with a lot of guns are hard to argue with. Those of us not participating in the violence tend to think that THEY will come to their senses and see the crimes of war that they are committing—someone somewhere. I think not. There isn't someone somewhere. There is only us.

The women of Liberia in West Africa realized this, that no one was going to save them from the male bloodlust, so they took on the Liberian government and the bands of brutal oppressors—stood up on the streets and didn't back down in the face of fearsome threats. Ellen Johnson Sirleaf led the *Women of Liberia Action for Peace* movement to win the 2005 elections, and in 2006 was inaugurated the first woman president in an African nation. Women can do it.

Primarily, men cannot be trusted to run the world for several main reasons:

1) Because men kill.

Not only do men kill other men and people in wars, but men kill people on the streets, the bars, the homes, and in their cars. They hunt animals for sport, they kill whales for money, they kill kill kill.

Uncle John says that "Murders have claimed more American lives during the 20th Century than wars have."
(More on this in Chapter 5).

2) Because men lose sight of priorities.

Many men support and avidly pursue the rights to take all and share nothing. In 2002, the company *Global Crossing* went bankrupt in the US leaving the bankruptcy legacy of loss for how many hundreds and thousands down the line while the CEO got $235M in stock options. $235M.

Enron executives and managers got $744M in 2001 before they went bankrupt leaving people with no pensions.

Tyco Stock Co lost $2.2M while the CEO received $80M in salary. Over three years, he made $300M and was then charged $1m for evading taxes. And he got paid all this while ruining the company. Another CEO was given a $10M severance package.

Bear Sterns went skidding down the greedy hill, but the CEO didn't suffer.

While these individual irresponsible men who deserved to be fired and jailed were pocketing their bonanza winnings, 17% of the white families in the USA had one parent (a mother), 54% of black families had only a mother, and 28% of the Hispanic families had only a mother. And single mothers, children, and old women are the largest segment of the impoverished in North America; they can't afford rent, health care or proper food.

Everyday we see the teenager or colored person who steals a car going to jail because thieves must be punished. If an executive or bigtime con artist steals the pension money of 10 000 old people who then live out their lives in poverty, he goes to live in Bermuda.

Nobody stops these men from taking everything and leaving nothing for the children or the mothers or the grandmothers of their children. Shame on them.

These systems would not survive if the male leaders in our patriarchy didn't approve of them. Our governments were set up to allow these crimes to go unpunished, because they were set up by the men who had much to gain from the system.

Seriously, let's stop tolerating the oppression, violence, and the killing. A PBS Frontline documentary on the Gulf War showed how brutal men can be with their macho long range weapons that melt the face of the enemy (the *enemy*—not human beings) onto the steering gear of their tanks. The Scud missile is not so clean as it blasts into fragments killing all the collateral people over a large area. Other weapons such as the Canadian-developed Supergun could stand well back of the returning flack and inflict big damage on the enemy sites. Aren't we clever?

That is what war is about, of course, killing more of them than they kill of us. To quote General Patton (a hero) "Kill as many of them as you can and as fast as you can." Such men become highly indignant when the young men they train to kill actually kill the wrong people. To wit, Noriega, bin Laden, the African tribesmen, Canadian, American, Russian soldiers, all soldiers—thinking of the My Lai massacre here. All soldiers are trained to kill, but don't always kill the *right* evil people. The *right* people change, of course.

And our clever scientists keep developing bigger and better weapons—huge Bertha bombs, and dirty bombs, and smart bombs, and megamegaton bombs—all of which our military leaders never expect to fall into the hands of the enemy. How not? The US developed the atom and hydrogen bombs but other countries are not allowed to defend themselves with those same bombs—only the US and maybe the British and the French can be trusted to bomb the right people with them, yet others less trustworthy have acquired them.

Try not to look at Bosnia or Rwanda and try to forget the Ethiopian, Somalian, Sudanese, Myanmar, Iraqi and Afghanistan atrocities while you wonder if the killing will ever stop. We have to consider how to stop the killing when every major country in the world is making a lot of money off the arms trade? How can we stop the biggest bullies in the world from buying, selling, and manufacturing arms when they have the weapons to intimidate any government who might choose to stand in front of the billion dollar export/import business? In December 2011, an explosion in Kabul killed 70 plus people. The Taliban claimed it was not a Taliban attack. Who then? Someone who had a lot of money to gain from continuing the war? The arms trade answers to no one.

On January 10, 2012, a French judge determined that the missile that brought down the Rwandan President's plane that sparked the Rwandan genocide was fired from a military camp. **It was not fired by Tutsi rebels**. He claims that extremist Hutus were to blame. Who hired the "extremist rebels"?

3) Because men are racist

Whatever the reason, men are usually more racist than women, and racism does not lead to peaceful coexistence, certainly not in a global world.

The male tribal urge to protect the tribe makes them suspicious of strangers or maybe in the competition for status and supremacy, they see other tribes as unknown quantities in the competition for their needs. Besides, they have seen collectively how the aboriginal tribes who treated strangers well (Canada, USA, Hawaii, Africa, Asia) were decimated for their generosity, so they recognize the need to challenge all comers.

And even when not outwardly racist, it seems much easier to kill people who look different—as apparently they don't embrace the same sense of loss when their relatives get killed, especially people with darker skin.

4) Because men are linear thinkers.

In most cases, men are linear thinkers (artists and musicians exempted), and the linear thinker sees a world that only goes in two directions, the one they choose and the one that opposes the one they choose. There are no other possibilities.

This is important.

Men see that they are going forward and if they are not going forward, they must be going backwards. If a person isn't on their side, on their team, then they must be on the other side; they must be the enemy.

After 9-11 in New York, President George W. Bush announced his war on terror, "You are either with us or against us." The absolute audacity and threat in that statement is staggering.

Many men think this way; there is good or there is bad. A heterosexual is good and a homosexual is bad, not noticing that pedophiles come in both orientations. She's a nice girl (that is, a girl who follows the rules men set out for her) or she's a slut is the Muslim/Christian/Judeo take. If men aren't winning, they must be losing. This is linear thinking of the very worst kind.

After the Sept 11 attacks, there was only one straight line response—retaliate. It doesn't matter if you don't know who to retaliate against, just pick someone and beat them up. It turned out to be Afghanistan and then Iraq because they both looked like easy fights—and they both have oil or a pipeline for the oil. And Afghanistan and Iraq didn't have any fighter jets to carry bombs across the Atlantic, and neither had the means to shoot down high-flying bombers. And the homeland wouldn't get damaged if the war was staged half a globe away.

Karate and Kung Fu are martial arts that demonstrate the power of the single-minded, the focused energy. The laser beam demonstrates the power of a concentrated little beam of light that can be a miraculous little tool, but it can also be used as a serious weapon. So, too, can otherwise helpful useful amazing men. When single-minded in destructive pursuits, using the laser strength of a singular focus, these leaders can pursue their ideologies at all costs.

With this linear approach to life that, on the positive side, enables men to achieve marvelous feats of engineering and technology, they are, unfortunately limited in their ability to see the full spectrum of possibilities and options. Most men are unable to see the whole picture, to see the kids in the foreground, the house and school behind them, the tree-covered hills bright in the clean air in the distance. They see a red Ferrari with a blonde woman at the wheel driving along the road in the middle distance—that's all they see. We would do well to look at the motivators of men to understand what makes them do what they do, as we do in chapter 2; then much of what we see in the world is more understandable.

Leadership requires the wisdom that comes from both sides of humanity, the male and the female. Do we want our babies to inherit a civilization of the brutes, where the cruelest men have the power and there are no safe places to live? Unbridled male behavior takes us down that road, and we are on that road.

(2) THE MALE NATURE

There are three main motivating factors involved in the human male behavior that I have been looking at:

- o   the procreative factor
- o   the dominator factor
- o   and the male hierarchy system
     (the pecking order)

All three are interdependent certainly, but can be seen in their separate aspects.

The Procreative Factor

Every male activity derives from the primal urge to procreate. This is not startling or unexpected: indeed, it is obvious.

It is, nevertheless, a most significant fact in which men are almost untouched by the evolution of the species. In other aspects, however, men are absolutely astounding at what they are capable of developing.

This huge paradox is responsible for the baffling behavior of the human being.

Men choose women who are beautiful, healthy, have good skin, have a wonderful shape, have sex appeal (suggesting reproductive readiness), are clean looking, are often smart and appear to have a marvelous gene pool. A TV documentary recently claimed that men are attracted to women who have the ratio of 7 to 10 from waist to hips as this is supposed to be the most desirable female proportion. This may be true. However, I don't know if we can believe that statement, since there is not a heterosexual man in the world, young or old, who is not a fool for a beautiful woman whether she has the magic ration of 7 to 10 or not, especially if she has attractive breasts.

In much of the English-speaking world, and Middle Eastern world, actually in most of the world, sex has taken on a very unhealthy women-debasing attitude. In the West, there is a proliferation of playboy titillation mentality that sees women as sex objects only and worthless in any other role. So if a woman is not as close to the ideal female as the men want, those women are scorned and belittled with a variety of ugly names. Women are not often encouraged to prepare themselves for the highest leadership positions.

What you worship is what you value, and if your society only worships the all-powerful male, then women have no status. Women either resent these sex object demands or they turn themselves inside out trying to meet those figments of skewed male imaginations, in some cases, actually starving themselves to death. If people esteemed both father and mother figures, then females would have value, and the needs of women and children would be met.

Jacquetta Hawkes wrote about the ancient Minoan society on Crete that seemed "to have reduced and diverted their aggressiveness through a free and well-balanced sex life."

Think about that observation in relation to our world that views sex as more sinful than violence and war. Jesse Ventura (a former wrestler and Governor in the US) said that he couldn't understand how President Clinton, who lied about his sex life could be impeached, and President Bush who lied about going to war wasn't impeached. We have the US public image demanding strict sexual behavior from their politicians and leaders, tearing them to pieces in their frenzies of righteousness, yet their daily public entertainment is slutty porn and hideous violence.

Where else can an Internet porn site make $20M in one year as one did in the US in 2001?

As a consequence, we have celibate priests reduced to perversion— good decent men so twisted in their emotional development that they break god-promised vows. How can such emphasis on such vows exact anything but confusion? You can't deny the most powerful human urge and not expect terrible consequences. Nowhere does Jesus deny procreation or sexual activities in the name of god—yet the Catholic Church leaders thrived on such power plays with their priests and followers.

Status & Position among Males

Briefly, men pursue their goals with awesome single-mindedness. The need to achieve enough status to be able to mate with the most desirable women in the world drives men in virtually every activity.

Look at these pursuits of status.

The cars, the technology, the military, the transportation provisions, the architecture, the market economy, all of these are in the pursuit of status on either smaller scales or grander scales.

Many men marry for decent regular sex, of course, but also to have status—the father of the family. Women believe their husbands marry them because they love them and that they are a team, a sharing unit in which their mutual good will determine the choices made in the marriage. And this is usually true. However, when it comes to love or status with a man, status usually wins. Salary and or status will determine the jobs he will take. Status will determine the activities he will agree to undertake and going to a child's birthday party is not high on the list as I noticed yesterday when my next door neighbor had a few families over to celebrate their 10year-old's birthday. The dads were not smiling as they got out of the cars.

Status & Competition—the game

Unlike Shakespeare's world where all the men and women are merely players in life's big drama, in the male world, all the men are competitors in a bunch of games. And the stakes in those games are absolute; they define who the men (and often the women) are in a very deep way. As spectators in a football match or a hockey game, if their team loses, they experience a real depression as though it was their own shame, as if their future will be lessened by the loss. Every endeavor is a competition and a serious competition.

Status rules. Status will determine whether a man will stay with the original wife. If he has earned all the status points and the trophy wife is the next achievement, the wife and kids are too often left in the suburbs.

Women generally do not understand these men. The wife of the CEO of Enron was interviewed on TV when the company first took a dive, and she protested over and over that her husband would never knowingly be party to the defrauding on people's pensions. She was wrong.

Women think they know men from their experiences with them as caring husbands, caring fathers, and pillars of the community; they do not know men from the core of their drives and motivations. Many men are almost split-brained in their responses to life. Under normal conditions, they are logical, engaging, responsible people, but when confronted physically or mentally or emotionally with the male challenge, real or perceived, they become unrecognizable. They are not rational, logical or reasonable. If a man is determined to get a certain status symbol or live in a style that reflects the kind of swaggering person he sees himself to be, then he is single-minded in getting it. The wife and the kids can go without as his ego needs pre-empt all. How many stories have we read of the alcoholic Irishman drinking his earnings "to be one of the lads" while his wife and kids starved?

Men believe that the status symbol among the boys gives him the procreative edge, even though it may mean dumping the family (his procreated descendants). Ultimately, the status pursuit takes on a life of its own and is the driving force that changes the gears in his ride through his life.

Many men become endorphin junkies, addicted to their self-esteem builders; they need the buzz and if the greater danger gives them a greater reward, then they will take on the greater danger without considering the consequences to anything but their own emotional-mental well being. They will climb Everest; they will dive off of cliffs; they will ski off of cliffs; they will risk all.

And what is the biggest challenge, the greatest danger? What is the most deeply scoring, deeply challenging activity in the world?
WAR.

The Male Dominator Role

Man's god-given right to oppress women and every other living being comes from a misguided Judeo idea:

"Man shall have dominion over all the beasts," and this is the BIG LIE.

This is the big lie that men bought with all their hearts and souls, a lie that has led civilization astray.

Somehow, the male interpretation of the beasts blurred over to include women, thanks to some misogynist early Abraham descendents, thus justifying the male oppression of women, animals, and all living things, as well as the planet's resources.

Most of the bible has been revised; there was the E (Elohim) revision, the J (Jesuit) revision, and the P (Priestly) revision to consolidate and justify the male intention to have dominion over all living things. But who can believe that a loving all-merciful god would order men to pillage and kill everyone in a village except the virgins who they were instructed to take for themselves to sell or enslave? Only someone whose own agenda is served by such preposterous claims.

The male world cosmology looks like this:

God
(who looks like a man and is an all-powerful male.)

Man
(who looks like god)

Woman
(servants of men &/or sex objects)

Animals
(food)

Living organisms
(greenery on the golf course)

Natural elements
(resources for industry)

Perhaps the cosmology should look more like this:

The Living Universe
Universal forces, both male and female

All living beings on the planet (female & male), including human and non-human animals and birds and fish.

Lower Life Forms plants that nourish the living

Elements that provide the nutrients for the plants

This cosmology, however, does not serve man's interests because it would lead people to recognize that they owe more to the survival of all living things than they owe to male ambition and the male god.

Instead, we have this worship of the male god who can hardly be denied because to do so is heretical and heretics can be killed, burned &/or tortured, and they were and are. Muslim and East Indian women who don't accept the male oppression can be killed; wives, sisters, daughters—they can all be killed by their male relatives because the women don't count in the eyes of the male who reveres a fear-provoking, inflexible, blood-lusting male god. The men in the Middle East have manufactured the evil of women, and they will destroy themselves in order to guarantee their right (divine right) to subjugate their women. They have to torment someone it seems.

There is a bitter irony here. If men let go of the religious lie, as many intelligent men have done, they find the respect they crave, the respect that has been denied them by their women and children who have lived in fear of them or are disgusted by them. If the men hanging on so tightly to the lie would relax, respect themselves and others, and have some fun without the onerous burden of keeping up the lie, their lives would be much happier.

The Male Hierarchy System

With the male pecking order system, we end up with a dangerous concentration of power that results in the impoverishing of most of the people.

Look at every country in the world to see proof of this pecking order in action—EVERY COUNTRY in the world, some in extreme, a few at near workable levels.

Men have a strange respect for the status pursuits of other men—an awe, perhaps, or a spectator respect to see how far the game is going to go even if they have to sacrifice their own lives for these other men's gains. It gets tangled up in *honor* that seems to be a motivating feature of the pecking order, that there is honor in performing your role without question when you are given a role in the order, even if it is a miserable role. War is the most obvious example.

And men can't seem to intrude on other men's games or limit the stakes in other men's games even when it hurts their own lives.

For example, look at fraternity hazing events. Ordinarily compassionate decent loving young men will sit and watch while other not-so-decent men humiliate and damage others, often women.

In war, when a group commits atrocities, the other men are often unwilling to intrude and stop the action because they "are following orders". Women, too, fall into this respect-the-alpha-leader mentality, but I think the women are simply following the male lead in these times and are not actually participating in any pecking order allegiance.

Men like the hierarchy system where they know their position, be it alpha, beta or omega, when their duties are clear, their allegiances are clear, their loyalties are blocked out for them.

I often say, don't follow others—they may be going to the dentist. They may be going where they really shouldn't be going, and they may be taking us all into our peril. Men don't find this to be an *honorable* attitude, however, and are willing to take the whole world into extinction in their allegiance to any presiding leader.

The pecking order system works to keep the alpha males, the King Rats, in power. This is the ultimate condition for procreation and survival of their own superior genes, controlling others to provide for themselves. The alpha males at the top of the order then ensure that the rest of the group is subservient and quiescent using any means that become necessary, more and more brutal if challenged. They will persuade, cajole, lie, cheat, bribe and then kill without remorse when answering their undisciplined primal lust.

Men create enemies when necessary, in order to rally the troops into a cohesive form that can be controlled and manipulated. All leaders know the power to be had in the creation of a dreadful common enemy that all must cooperate to defeat. [Pol Pot in Kapuchea (Cambodia) managed to make intellectuals the enemy.] And with that unquestioned cooperation, they are free to do whatever they like without criticism. Often, they have to manufacture the enemy or the fear or set up a

Tonkin incident or a Weapons-of-Mass-Destruction fear or spread the rumor that some uneasy alliance group has committed an atrocity that must be avenged. Then you have a situation ripe for the glorious leader to take the dominant oppressor position.

The boy's club is the linchpin of the whole system that keeps the wheels of the machine turning over so that their King Rat stays in power. The alpha males need the King Rat to ensure their boy's club survives in order to keep themselves in the status (wealth) position. The members of the club usually do not take public office, and we don't always recognize these members in their day to day activities, but it works well, and the honor system is not violated without serious consequences.

One example of the workings of the King Rat and the boy's club happened in Canada when one of the richest families in Canada wanted to take several billion dollars out of the country in direct violation of the law. Mulroney's government turned a blind eye, and might have instructed the Income Tax dept to do so also. We will never know. The crime was pointed out to the succeeding Prime Minister, Jean Chretien, who promised an investigation, which, of course, dragged along, if indeed it was even started, and the whole issue dropped out of sight by the time the time limit for blocking the move was up. The media, being one of the major movers in the Boy's club, and the RCMP, at the time being reduced to a beta position under the direction of the boy's club, all assisted in losing $6M of the people's money in taxes in that instance.

So we may think we have democracy, that our governments will serve the people, that we have the right to vote the bad guys out and put good guys in, but it doesn't work that way. We get to vote for different-looking guys but they all do the same thing because they don't get elected if they don't sit down to brunch at the boy's club.

Women have been conditioned to uphold the male hierarchy system as well. They have their place and they don't break out of it. Some of us that do are either firmly put back into our place or we are dismissed. But women can rise to the occasion when their contribution is valued.

When doing research for this book, one small example of female conditioning became apparent. I went to the Women's Studies department at the university where I was lecturing, and asked the secretary for some help. She asked me what I needed, and then she offered some very useful directions and suggestions, writing down titles and names of authors for me. She was very self-assured, forthright, and well versed in everything I wanted to know.

When I went to the science departments, the secretaries upheld the male hierarchy order by trying to think of which professor would be able to help me, not offering any help of their own. There are certainly female professors in the sciences, but I was forcefully struck by the acceptance of "place" in the hierarchy of the science secretaries who showed no personal sense of their ability to contribute, in marked contrast to the women's studies' secretary who was fully actualized as a person.

This surely is what this male-dominant society is doing—it is undermining a female's sense of competence, and it is distorting and crippling males as well. The whole system is destructive to all its inhabitants, human or not, as well as the planet.

We have been brought up to follow the leader—we even had childhood games of Follow the Leader—and thanks to that edict, we had good church-going men and women in Germany torturing and killing Jews by the millions. Did they think Hitler was god, he who must be obeyed, the divine leader who must be followed?

In our society, people follow the leader with great devotion and force their children to do so also. The Jehovah Witness children are actively discouraged from pursuing an education—very very few go to college or university. One student told me of a young Jehovah Witness girl to whom she was giving piano lessons, which the girl loved with all her heart. The girl's family stopped the lessons *for the girl's own good*. The leaders did not approve. And it goes on and on under the oppression of ignorant men and their allegiance to the hierarchy.

On the larger scale, we have Pakistan and India and Iraq and Iran following the lead set by the West in developing nuclear bombs. Better they follow us to the dentist.

They all need a new direction to follow. Peace—it used to be a word people believed in.

Women in the Pecking Order

While many people gain a sense of belonging and a sense of their place in the social structure by following leaders, women and many men as well feel terribly undervalued in this oppressive hierarchy. Their worthwhile ideas are ignored because they are only "workers", and the lower administrators are at the mercy of some intimidated or mean-minded higher administrators who are themselves disillusioned with the Board of Directors they must answer to, and up and down it goes.

Many creative men and women are not hustlers by nature and are at a terrible disadvantage in a world constructed on the pecking order where only the hustler gets heard and hired. If they can't find someone to hustle for them, their talents are never utilized, and some of the best minds and most talented artists are wasted because the hierarchy has only 2 directions, up and down.

Men are generally very uncomfortable in the presence of really strong women since these women are not part of the male strata system, and they don't know where the women fit. They would just as soon eliminate them from the decision-making equation and many actively try to do so. This is much like the English with their class system in which the English don't know where North Americans fit in their class structure, so some of them put us all on a lower rung since we don't have a "place" clearly defined; others treat us with amusement.

Similarly, men feel that women intruding into the male zone is a threat to male supremacy: they fear being dominated in an order that is not conforming to their established system. But having strong women in the society does not mean female domination. Women don't particularly fear very intelligent male leaders (when they come across one)—they respect them. Women fear the thugs, the powerful ego-centric male who has bought the Big Lie, and who does not respect the female status or contribution.

Also, men should rejoice in the presence of strong intelligent women because those are the women who will make sure the children are well brought up, and who will ensure the men's dignity will be respected in ill health and old age.

Testosterone and Decision Making

In April, 2008, researchers at the University of Cambridge released a study of traders in the City of London financial district that showed that male traders made bigger profits on days when their testosterone levels were high. This study suggested that testosterone may help focus the mind but *constantly high testosterone levels are likely to make traders foolhardy.*

"Rising levels of testosterone and cortisol prepare traders for taking risk," said John Coates, who led the study. "However, if testosterone reaches physiological limits, as it might during a market bubble, it can turn risk-taking into a form of addiction, while extreme cortisol during a crash can make traders shun risk altogether."

These Cambridge researchers found that daily testosterone was significantly higher on days when traders make more than their one-month daily average. Whether the higher levels contributed to the success outcomes or whether the levels were higher *because* they were so successful was not mentioned in the news report of this study. It could be either way.

However, the Cambridge researchers did report that their work suggested that the rapid decisions the traders were pressured to make may be biased by emotional and hormonal factors that have not so far been considered in any detail. Coates said that this bias may help explain both rational and irrational behavior.

Can we extrapolate this to apply to government leaders? Because this could account for the almighty necessity to maintain the political leaders' seats in government for which they sell their souls. They are addicted to the hormonal effects of high-level decision making. But these decisions can be compromised by their emotional and hormonal levels.

Power corrupts says the old cliché, which is absolutely true; however, power both compromises and corrupts. Former US President Bill Clinton started out with good intentions—health care that got squashed as a consequence of a huge campaign of lies by the insurance companies and the medical industry who are getting fat on sick Americans. In 2007, a report showed that the US has the most expensive health care system in the world and it does not provide the best care. Clinton was trying to do a good thing. Then several years later, President Clinton ended up handing over the digital air wave spectrum to the media giants for nothing when it could have been *leased* for $70Billion which would go a long way in getting the health care program up and running.

Speaking of the lies that the insurance companies and the health industry propagated in that health care campaign. Advertisers on American TV are not allowed to broadcast lies about the products they sell, but the political candidates and their super-paks can broadcast blatant lies in their TV attack ads with impunity. The Swift Boat ads against John Kerry when he was running for President stand out. This is another case where the leaders and would-be leaders can be as corrupt as they choose to be.

It would seem that the stronger the male dominance, the more corrupt the society. In India, corruption is rampant. Edward Luce wrote that nearly a fifth of parliament members have been indicted for at least one crime,

> "Many people, especially foreigners, do not appreciate the extent of corruption in India . . . they think it is an additional nuisance to the system . . . in many parts of India *it is* the system."

Very few people can resist the temptations of power. We think fondly of former Prime Minister of Canada (now deceased) Pierre Trudeau because he was a man who was strong enough to withstand the destructive addiction of power. He never lost sight of the fact that the man in the limelight was a dramatic role he was playing on the world stage—not his real life person.

So men are not better decision makers than women. Indeed, they have conflicting hormonal influences at work in their decision-making. Surely the Cambridge study by Dr. Coates helps us understand how men in power can get so far off the rails with their original decent intentions, and why they need women who are not testosterone driven to participate in the leadership of the communities, cities, and nations.

(3) MEN & FINANCIAL RESPONSIBILITY

In John Robert Colomba's 1996 Canadian Global Almanac, he writes,

> "The Canadian International Development Agency (CIDA) includes women in their aid efforts, recognizing that development is impossible without the participation of half the world's population, particularly the half that has the bulk of the responsibility for health care, education and agriculture."

We have to read that last part again, "particularly the half that has the bulk of the responsibility for health care, education and agriculture."

For what, then, does the other half have responsibility?

Well, other than health, education, and food, there is shelter, aaaaaaand there are male toys and male games. Males toys cost a lot of money in the patriarchal society—in fact, most of the world's money goes to producing, selling, and buying those boy's toys and funding the male games.

In 2003, the largest per cent of women in BC—29.3% earned under $10,000.

The 2nd largest—27.5% of women earned under $20,000.

Almost 60% of women earned under $20,000. That is poverty.

The largest percent of men in BC—21.9%—earned over $50,000, while only 6.3% of BC women earned over $50,000.

Clearly all the products and all the services in a market society will be designed for those with the money to buy those products—that is, men earning over $50,000 because it is smart business to sell one item for $70,000 than to sell 70,000 at $1. For the men between the ages of 35-60 years who make up the bracket that earns over $50,000, we have cars, cars, cars, boats, boats, boats, and lots of recreational toys, executive travel, electronic computers, games and tools, and war, always war, and mega sports. Men have no conscience about the unlimited amounts of money they squander on sports every day while pregnant women in Brooklyn are breathing in toxins—PCBs—that guarantee their children will be learning disabled.

Even in health care, men spend the money on themselves. In one year in the US, $12B was spent on heart bypass surgery. According to Dr. Dean Ornish, *91% of those surgeries* were done on white upper middle class males, even though heart disease affects as many women as males. In 2011, however, there were questions about the efficacy of those surgeries.

Looking at a couple of male interests is an education in budget priorities. How about car racing?

Formula 1 car racing:

Ten years ago the cost of the cars for one race team (for 4 race cars not including the test team cars) for one year was well over $52M based on some British American Racing (BAR team) numbers. This $52M is only a fraction of the cost of racing these cars because it does not include the millions of dollars in salaries for the drivers and the team, nor does it include the traveling and hotel expenses or the uniforms or insurance, design, research and development, crashes, fuel and oil, etc. The stickers that they stick on the cars for advertising cost $1500.

This is only one team of perhaps 10 teams.
Ten teams = **$527M.**
And that was 10 years ago.

There are many motor-racing divisions as well. There is the Indy car racing league, the CART racing league, the Indy Lights racing league, the F1A, the motorcycle supercross racing league, the Motorcycle AMA formula Xtreme Series, the USAAAR hooters pro Cup Series auto racing, the SCCA Pro Rally auto racing, the NHRA Drag Racing Series, the Toyota Atlantic Racing Series, and the NASCAR racing league that probably spends more money than all the other leagues put together. All these racing series attract huge crowds who buy big buck tickets at big venues, mostly to watch vehicles go around in a circle for a couple of hours.

We could look at the expenses for baseball competition, hockey competition, golf and football competition and come up with equally mind-boggling expenses. We can't even mention Monster Truck competitions that attract 70,000 paying spectators at their events.

In the basketball leagues, some of the salaries could support whole communities. In the NBA, Kevin Garnet made $22.4M one season. He made over $22M in one year—*to play basketball.*

The New York Knicks doled out slightly more than $85M in salaries in 2002; *$19M for players no longer with the team.*

War games

If we want to look at the really big expensive games that men play, however, we have to look at the war games. The war games, by their very important nature, go outside of all bounds of practicality, reason, and accountable results. In the name of war, men have carte blanche to spend like bi-polar patients on an all time manic high. Nothing can take precedence over war (and Cold War) spending, and none of it needs to be made public. Supplying weapons and supplies for war is the perfect greed arrangement.

Is it any wonder that the richest people in the world are into military supplies in which they have no competition (single-sourced, it is called), are accountable to no one for the quality and reliability of their products, and can set any profit margin they choose. The weapons don't even have to work as apparently none of the anti-ballistic missiles did.

In the almanacs of facts, you won't find arms or weapons in the imports and exports, yet all the developed nations are involved in the arms trade. We do know, however, that the world military expenditures have been estimated at $798 Billion in the year 2000. That is a lot of beans,—approximately 798,000,000,000 cans of baked beans actually.

The United States of America is the major arms exporter in the world. Between 1993-1997, the US govt sold, approved or gave away $190B in weapons to most nations in the world. In 1992, the US supplied arms or military technology to more than 92% (39 of 42) of the wars being waged at the time. The US taxpayer has, at times, paid the cost of some of these sales. For example, the US sold military merchandise in 1996 to Romania (a seriously cash-strapped country). If they were to default on their payment, the US taxpayers would pay the $16.7M loss but the manufacturer, United Industrial, would get paid.

The money involved in war and weapons carries a lot of muscle in government. The top lobbyist in the 2000 election cycle in the US was Lockheed Martin (putting up $2.38M); they were also the top defense contractors in the US with contracts to the tune of $15.1B. After Sept 11, General Dynamics got a $6M contract from the US Navy on May 21, and on May 30, they got another $11M contract from the US govt. Not bad business this war business. And later, Iraq became the sugar daddy of wars.

[I use the USA for these examples because there are hard facts available on the US expenditures and activities—thanks to their previously more open policy on information. Other countries— all other countries in Europe, in Asia, South America, and Africa,—are all just as irresponsible with the taxpayer's money. So, though it may look like I am condemning the US (in their self-designated role as the world leader, I could do so) they are just one country in many making huge profits in the arms trade, in instruments of killing others and killing us when those other nations turn these weapons they bought from us against us.

Every government given the power the US now has would be just as irresponsible and corrupt because they are all run by competitive men. [Even if the leader is a woman, they are run by men.]

This arms industry is surely a crime against humanity. Even when there isn't a war, many nations engage in warlike behavior with their espionage activities and their preventative arms buildup. They don't need a war to commandeer all the money the workers generate. There are several outstanding cases that have been documented by way of examples here.

During the Cold War in the 60s, the US spent $17B putting microphones around all the world's oceans listening for Russian submarine activity, a "classified" budget decision. Of course, anti-communism was still a mighty fear factor that justified this paranoia. The US Congress may have ponied up the $17B to keep the communist dogs at bay or maybe they weren't required to approve such defense measures.

The dreaded communist party in the US that was such a threat to the Americans consisted "largely of FBI agents" Attorney General Robert Kennedy said, but the creation of an enemy served to rally support behind the leaders even if the bad guys were themselves.

The Soviets were equal opponents in this spy game. The Americans found many miles of the underwater northern Soviet communication line and put listening devices under 1200 miles of the Soviet cable. They believed the Soviets did not know they were listening in on all Soviet fleet directives since the Soviets could repair and maintain their lines without detecting the listening devices. However, the Russian spy, Ronald Pelton, had tipped the Russians to the listening devices who then transmitted phony information back to the Americans, and thus another $3B was wasted. If you put in the 0s of $3B, it looks like this: $3,000,000,000. A lot of money for some old boys' games.

The US also spent over $200M (no one knows how much over) trying to raise a sunken Russian nuclear submarine armed with 3 nuclear missiles in the waters off Hawaii. The US wanted to steal this sub, the K129, but trying to lift it was one huge engineering feat—the challenge for which no cost would be spared. They had Howard Hughes build a 619foot megaton ship, (55,000-63 000 tons, depending on the source). Every part of this Hughes *Glomar Explorer* was custom built with a huge claw the size of a football field, winches, decontamination areas, etc. to raise the submarine. Hughes kept it all secret, for which he held the Navy ransom.

Using the *Glomar Explorer*, the US navy tried to lift the submarine but didn't secure the sub on the first try. They did not take the time to assess the damage on this first try, and on the second try, they succeeded in lifting the submarine, but half way up, three of the claws (previously damaged) let go and the nuclear torpedo that was sitting loose in one tube slid out and dropped onto the ocean floor—and apparently did not explode. Some reports say none of the code books or torpedoes were recovered and other reports say the code books and the other two nuclear torpedoes were recovered.
The press got word of it, so the *Glomar Explorer* was moth-balled for almost 20 years before being refitted in 1998 as an oil drilling ship. And another $200M was wasted.

The Russians and the Americans were chasing each other all over the world's oceans in their male games of one-up-man-ship, risking serious nuclear war. One time the Russians did fire a torpedo at a US ship which apparently outran the torpedo. Commander Richard Compton-Hall, a retired Royal Navy commander, commented on the Nova TV show, *Submarines, Secrets and Lies,* that it was "like cowboys and indians and later more like 3 dimensional chess."

The games, the games.

Chief Seattle, a First Nation's person who lived in Washington State before it was Washington State, was a man who saw much of the greed and ruthlessness of men who were set on "getting ahead" and dominating those who got in their way. He said, back in 1855:

> "Young men are impulsive. When our young men grow angry at some real or imaginary wrong, and disfigure their faces with black paint, it denotes that their hearts are black, and then they are often cruel and relentless, and our old men and old women are unable to restrain them. Thus it has ever been. Thus it was when the white men first began to push our forefathers further westward . . . Revenge by young men is considered gain,

even at the cost of their own lives, but old men who stay at home in times of war, and mothers who have sons to lose, know better."

There is much to consider in that statement because older men with ambition know that all they have to do is sow the seeds of some "real or imaginary" wrongs, and the young men will take up arms and kill for them—at the cost of their own lives. And these men whose hearts are black are also extremely irresponsible and waste humongous amounts of money on their killing ventures. The Serbs were told the lie that the Croats had killed Serb babies, and this "imaginary wrong" launched a genocide.

How else to use up old weaponry if you don't have wars? You may have to start wars if necessary to get those lucrative military contracts to restock newer weapons. And all those military commanders with their medals puffed out on their chests become very important.

Business

Business is the obvious stage for financial irresponsibility because the purpose of most businesses now is to GET money, not necessarily to meet a need as blacksmithing, tire repair, or tool manufacturing used to be. Most businesses now are designed to produce and sell whatever will make money. Using advertising, business *creates* a need for their products, products that hopefully will be obsolete in a short time. Think computer devices.

On April 1, 2003, the BC Government hired a Bermuda-based company, Accenture, to run many of BC Hydro's "back-office functions, representing approximately 1500 employees . . . These functions include Business Support Services, Customer Services, Human Resource Services, Building and Office Services, Payroll and Accounts Payable Services, Financial Systems Services and Purchasing Services." Accenture is "a global management consulting technology services and outsourcing company helping clients become high-performance businesses and governments." Incredibly, we don't have 1500 individuals in BC who can do these jobs for our own power company. As Accenture claims, "Outsourcing has succeeded because of its ability to reduce risk, drive standardization, increase productivity, and improve reliability and predictability—in other words, its ability to industrialize an ever-increasing range of business activities." Essentially, they help big companies who don't want to pay taxes to support the countries where they are protected by laws that ensure honest business.

It is not that we do business in other countries that is a problem, such business is good for the world, but when companies do business in other countries in order to cheat their own country, then it becomes reprehensible.

Businesses engage in corporate wars for financial supremacy. These business warriors steal from the competition, force competitors out of business with business mergers, and "win" in stock swindles. In Dan Brown's book "Digital Fortress", one of the characters says "Business is war—and war was exciting." Very clever is the modern financial warrior in his ability to cheat and destroy, and win the spoils.

Our governments actively engage in the interests of big business by brokering big trade agreements with other countries. John R. MacArthur, the publisher of Harper's, said that

> "The point [of these Agreements] is to allow American corporations to operate as cheaply as possible in foreign countries and to protect them from expropriation and seizure of assets."

He cites Ohio as one state that has been devastated by the NAFTA agreement.

These agreements have largely laid out the rules for business wars that answer to the financial tribunals, those who control (maybe not run) the World Trade Organization, the World Bank, and the International Monetary Fund. By holding the whole world ransom, these powerful directors suck the wealth out of the people, and the forests, fields, and oceans—by simply squeezing the politicians. With a few threats and bribes, the leaders we elect hand the countries over to these renegade financiers who don't even get off their horses.

For example, in 1995, Canada overspent on infrastructure projects (at least that is what we were told, though you couldn't see the evidence when driving down the road) and the International Monetary Fund (IMF) sent a letter telling the Canadian government what to do about it: specifically, to cut back on the health care funding, the education funding and the welfare programs and that is exactly what the government did. No other alternatives were even suggested. Jeopardizing the health of the people was not an issue if the money people told the government to do so.

Currently, the trade representatives are forcing third world countries to "open their markets" as Canada and Mexico have done, give up their resources, and accept so-called development that destroys their ability to be self-supporting, forcing them into debt purchasing the commodities they can no longer grow or manufacture for themselves.

One of the most soul-searing pictures I ever saw was on TV during the war in Somalia. The film showed a long line of starving refugees walking along a road in their own country, children, men, and women, many of them old people, with as many of their belongings as they could carry—*walking past huge plantations of food on both sides of the road.*

These people were starving to death walking past plantations of food growing in their own country—food grown for export and profit.

They would have been shot if they had helped themselves to feed their babies.

I thought that this must have been how the Irish looked as they starved in the 1850s while food was being shipped out of Ireland to markets in England. Not something you quickly forget.

There is much evidence all over the world that men do not provide adequately for wives and children whether the family is together or separated. This is because men in most families decide how the money will be spent, and their own personal interests always come first.

Somehow we have to modify the male urge to spend all for themselves. We must infuse the role of caretakers of the human race and planet with more appeal. We must promote the honor and glory to be gained by men who compete with each other to have the best cared-for family.

Taxes

The tax systems have been developed by males. Currently, where I live, I pay 25-30% income tax when I get the money, I pay 25-30% on the interest if I keep the money (even if I only get 2% interest), and I pay 12% more when I spend the money. The only thing I see for this money is congestion on the roads, and garbage pickup, except they don't pick up wood, gyproc, metal, disposable diapers, etc.etc. (Since I don't have a pickup truck I am not sure where I am supposed to put these things.) The government gets most of the money I work for, obviously, and often they use that money to bail out incompetent rich people.

Cheating on taxes is considered to be very clever. And men who have control of so much more money to cheat with, make sure they elect governments who won't waste that money on the moms and kids. How honorable is that to be one of the lads that cheats women and kids?

Big companies set up tax shelters off shore and claim their right to do so saying they can't compete and keep the prices down for the consumer if they have to pay huge taxes. It is all done for our benefit—lower prices.

Wasting all the money has gotta stop.

(4) MEN & HONOR
(LOSING OR NOT LOSING FACE)

Men have determined what is honorable and they pride themselves on serving that sense of honor. We all love the man who protects the wife and kids—who takes on the honorable role in defense of a good thing. But much honor is empty image-making. Women are not so caught up with the honor-image-status thing.

Men are keeping their honor safe when most of us have no idea the man is doing this.

For example:

One couple broke up, astounding their friends. "But he loved you and thought so much of you. He was just telling us how well you were doing in the business course," they told the wife. But he would drive home from a gathering where he had been praising the wife to others and not say one word to her, walk down the hall to his room, and shut the door for the night.

Obviously, he either wanted to be seen as the fortunate man who had married a wonderful woman or he wanted to be seen as a man who was generous of spirit—a magnanimous gentleman. The image to men is so much more important than the reality.

How many men have refused to learn things that would make them successful or happy because they didn't want to appear to be a duffer—for some misguided sense of image.

For example: one young woman was teaching water-skiing in the summers. She had a class of both males and females, and on the first day they were taking their nosedives. One of the young men said he wanted to try skiing barefoot. She tried to tell him that it was much harder and that he should try the skis first. But he was adamant. So she told him how to do it and he tried and failed. But they all clapped, and he felt like he had succeeded because he had failed at something impossible, but he hadn't taken the risk of failing at something that many of them were learning successfully—he didn't lose face. But he also didn't learn to waterski. He sabotaged himself for the sake of his self-image.

Women are much more pragmatic—we don't have the big *honor* burden, though men impose it on us. The Muslim men and East Indian men kill their women if they decide the woman has dishonored the family—or if they want to justify getting rid of them. Of course, the men have decided what conduct will be a dishonor to the family. Strange that killing doesn't dishonor the family or dishonor their religion or their country. By some twist, killing is honorable among these spoiled male children.

A young 30 year old East Indian mother, Manjit Panghali, a kindergarten teacher was killed here on the outskirts of Vancouver in November, 2006, and her body was burned and dumped on the jetty of a port terminal 4 miles from my home. A month later, her 35 year old husband, Mukhtiar Panghali, was charged with her death, and his 27 year old brother, Sukhvinder Panghali was charged as an accessory after the fact and with interfering with a dead body. The husband was a high school teacher. The couple had both gone to university here, and they had a 3 year old daughter. The young woman was 4 months pregnant when she was killed.

This beautiful much-loved kindergarten teacher was the third young East Indian woman to die in the area in this brutal fashion in a two month period. These men are thugs. One has to wonder if civilization has evolved at all in the last 10,000 years. Such men pretend to be civilized with their cell phones, with photo downloads and their tailored clothes covering up a very poor excuse for a human being.

The image that men so deeply live for often manifests as an obsession with honor. The New Yorker Magazine had an article on dueling in the March 12, 2007, issue written by Arthur Krystal. The first person to ban dueling was a woman, Queen Isabella of Spain in 1480. And the Roman church decreed in 1563 that all duelists were to be excommunicated. But these laws were not effective and dueling continued. Krystal wrote in his article that among the gentry in the Middle Ages, almost every offense became an offense against honor. He noted that "Two Englishmen dueled because their dogs had fought."

Fortunately, by 1844, another woman, Queen Victoria, had had enough, and imposed harsh punishment on any officer involved in a duel, and Prime Minister Robert Peel supported the move with further penalties. What is such twisted honor? It appeals to a male sense of drama, bravado, macho in every way. However, as Krystal wrote, "Men not killed outright could die in great pain from ruptured organs and suppurating infections." That doesn't look like such an honorable death.

In ancient times, men sacrificed humans to appease their gods. They somehow believed God would be happy to see them kill one of His children. The Aztec leaders in the 14thC told their followers that if they stopped the sacrifice of virgins, their civilization would collapse.

Muslim, Christian, Hindu, almost any religion other than Buddhism is composed of men who have been or are bent on holy wars. Honorable men killing for the love of God. Many of these same men are rabidly anti-abortion and even anti-birth control. But killing grown humans for God the creator is honorable.

The need to save face is very upfront in many male societies. Japan is particularly identified but it is not just the Asian countries that have to save face. Losing face for many men is perhaps the greatest disgrace a man could suffer and in Japan (and Wall Street) was vitiated by the honorable suicide, honor for the sake of honor. Losing face was an honorable reason for killing someone or starving a group of people to death, more important than providing food and shelter for their families.

In the West, we also have this male loss of face predicament both nationally and individually. If a woman plays a game against a man and wins once, he will be gracious and generous (some men will). If the woman beats him repeatedly, he will lose his goodwill and soon will resent her and will find her company less than desirable. To avoid these ugly repercussions, women will avoid playing games against men when they know they can win.

And this male loss of face issue is determining the survival of the whole species at the moment as the US seeks face-restoring respect after the Sept 11 attacks, and face-saving revenge on Saddam Hussein as they have with Castro of Cuba.

So self-important such men are. Losing face is symptomatic of a huge ego that can't cope with a slight or a failure. If two people compete, for heaven sake, *one has to lose.* But next time, maybe, the loser will win and the other person will lose. But if the foolish honorable one kills himself, he will never know. Their families would have benefited from a little less of this honor. You didn't see Japanese women immolating themselves on a sword, (though they did commit suicide for other reasons.)

And you didn't see women in Europe dueling with pistols. All this honor nonsense is an ape chest-pounding characteristic, though perhaps I malign the ape.

Also, of course, men have convinced themselves that it is honorable to fight for one's country. All rights and needs must be sacrificed "for the country". (And incidentally, for themselves in some cases to make huge amounts of money.) Many of these countries are not worth fighting for. Is it honorable to fight for one's country as so many hundreds of thousands did for Hitler and Germany? Do any of these people fighting today really understand what they are killing for? Once they sign up, they take an oath to follow orders. How convenient. Then they need take no responsibility for the killing. And the hyenas who give the orders don't take responsibility either.

Women also want the money and the status but we shouldn't confuse these wants with some misguided sense of honor or image. They simply want to look sexy, and to secure the comforts and the prestige and the security the money will provide for their pleasures and for raising the children. Women make a lot of difficult choices in order to provide their offspring with advantages so that they will flourish in this world.

Denying women the freedom of movement and speech, their rights to choose how they live, how they will dress, how they will get educated, how they will choose a husband, and abusing them with impunity is not honorable. And the men that force these conditions on women are a scourge on the human race, with their perverted "honor" for men who don't want to look after themselves. No man will give up slaves willingly, and these men who wear the shield of religion and righteousness appropriate to themselves the right to enslave women. Loving god has nothing to do with abusing, subjugating and killing their women.

It takes a secure, mature, reasonable man to accord women their proper status in the world and to take the responsibilities to protect that.

(5) MEN & COMPETITION

The problem here with male rule is that it is all about competition—not cooperation, not mutual support for the common good and their own good—but competition. And this competition is tied up with status and image just discussed in Chapter 4.

So we have men racing cars that kill, motorbikes that kill, hang-gliding in more and more peril that kills, all the racing sports that imperil their lives. Succeeding in these pursuits is a huge endorphin high and self-enhancing esteem builder. We have men trekking to the north pole, the south pole, and Mt Everest—there is currently a very large industry in Nepal meeting the needs of thousands of trekkers climbing to base camp, climbing Annapurna, and hiking the Himalayas. Apparently the garbage is a big problem.

We have boys riding motocross bikes and skateboards up and down cement stairs, on cement ledges, up and down park benches, all brain-smashing risks. What is the reward?—the endorphin high, the male ego satisfaction, proving to themselves that they can take on the challenges that will come to them—proving their manhood.

Women can do these things (and some men can't) but women don't achieve the same rewards. There was a series on PBS TV, a British series, "Why Men Don't Iron," an investigation into the male and female responses to various activities. The conclusions were that the stress of those daring death-defying activities gave men a big endorphin lift, a huge surge of life-affirming well being, whereas the same games and challenges gave women mostly unpleasant energy-sapping stress.

Survival of the species builds competition into the DNA of the species, you insist. Well, yes. There were dangers out there and the fleetest of foot, the strongest physique, the most accurate bow and arrow artist would have a greater chance at the food supply. But now we don't run across the savannah after a gazelle. We don't fight off the bear in the berry patch.

But men have the raging competitive gene with no hand to hand competitor within range. It is hard to wrestle a computer.

So to assuage this competitive component of the survival instinct that has run amok, men compete in and for everything. "If I get more than the next guy, I'll survive and maybe he won't. I'll get the money, then I will get the supermodel, and she will have superior children, and . . ."

However, this competition is not ensuring man's survival; it is guaranteeing the extinction of the race. When the competition gets going, men are blind to the consequences (like gamblers) and ALL is at stake, ALL. And if it takes nuclear weapons to best the bastards, believe me, they are going to use them.

Under male leadership, *everything* has become a competition. Take a look at the food industry. Just the words *food industry* are masculine and don't smack of warm kitchens with the soup pot bubbling. Food comes to us in every unnatural form possible—for the benefit of profit and someone else's survival, not our health.

The Money Race

Men also approach the world of business as a big competition to be won or lost with the winner taking the spoils. The bigger the company, the bigger the rake-off of the spoils.

This money race is killing us. We aren't all financial athletes, skilled psyche players in the big get-everyone's-money race, yet we all have contributions to make to society if we get the opportunities to make those contributions instead of being forced to run a race we can't win.

A single woman I know runs a pottery studio. She teaches beginning and intermediate level, hand building and wheel work. She has a class of wheelchair students from the nearby rehab center, another class is brain-injured students, and there are classes of elementary school students and other young and old and foreign students, all learning to create with their hands, learning self esteem, camaraderie, skills, and appreciation for art. At home this woman has a son who was brain injured in an oil rig accident in Alberta, who the doctors said would die by the time he was 30, but at 38 he still suffers and makes her suffer with his brain-injured anger. Her 80-year-old mother also lives with her. She has a big investment in Shimpo wheels, kilns, thousands of dollars in glazes and all the other equipment, shelving, and display cases. Last month she didn't make the rent—summer is unpredictable, and she is not covering expenses, and, of course, people continually take more than they are entitled to. She is a 59 year old nervous wreck. No amount of hard work will make any difference. She is so distressed over the defaulted rent, expecting someone to walk in and shut her down any day, that she is physically ill, unable to hold food down. This remarkable humanitarian's contribution to the community seems to have no value,—unlike the business next door that is thriving selling shock absorbers. She does not have the necessary aptitude to run successfully in the competitive money race, so she is dispensable.

Sports

Men and sports go together like beef and gravy. Is there ever one without the other?

As in all other endeavors that men pursue in their single-minded fashion, sports takes on a mega importance that justifies tremendous expenditures of energy and time and money. Huge amounts of money go to buy the gear (the cars, the uniforms, the scoring mechanisms, the timing devices, the scuba equipment, the climbing tackle, the fishing tackle, the surfing boards, the sail planes, the soccer shoes, the skis and ski passes), the venues, (the arenas, the stadiums, the fields, the waterways, the marinas, the stands), the SUVs to get them to the sport locations, the expenses of the participants and the spectators, the media coverage,—massive industries once again to achieve the power and the glory or at least watch when others get the power and the glory.

The family takes second place when a man has to watch *his game*. Women understand this part of the male behavior since it has ever been, and many women even contribute to the enjoyment of these male games by going with the men to the games or providing the snacks in front of the TV. They hope that the male's preferred team will win so that he will be in a good mood after the game. Men identify their own self-esteem with the players they root for, and a loss by *their team* is a personal loss. This is not so hard to understand, this identification with the home team, except now there are no more home teams as the players are global and keep switching teams for more money.

We have the big money sports, the yachting and the heli-skiing come to mind and the $1M yacht is not such a rarity. I saw a yacht for sale on TV the other day—solid teak panelling, millwork with 6 coats of varnish, and it gets 2 ½ miles per gallon (diesel). If all those yachts in the marinas were actually in action very often, the pollution and inefficiency would be enormous. Yachting, of course, is also a competition.

Participating in sports is a good thing for men. Men need the endorphin boosters of the physical activities, and the camaraderie with other men to keep them stable. What is now bad about sports is the invasion of the money merchants,—the big business operators who have turned the sports into big business that puts much of the action out of reach of the common people here in the West.

Throughout Europe and South America there are the pick up soccer games going on at all times and all ages participate in many different locations.

But in the West, many sports are now largely spectator sports. And even the spectator aspect has become difficult for many of the men and boys. A dad taking his son to a hockey game in Vancouver costs well over a hundred dollars. These sports are mostly enjoyed by those who work for companies who buy season tickets, and when they are lucky they get to use the company tickets. One corporation supports another corporation and calls it sport.

Hockey has become such a cash cow that now a season's ticket does not get you into the playoffs which is another whole series of games—the quarter finals, the semifinals and eventually the finals. But if you have a season's ticket, then you get FIRST dibs on buying the playoff season's tickets. And in the world of male competition, if it is first for anything, you just line up. So you buy two series of tickets to actually see the season's series of games.

The TV coverage of sports events has also become an exercise in angst as most of the interesting plays happen during the endless commercials, and the viewer sees the game or race mostly on instant replays or dizzying fast frame editing or partially on the screen while the network runs banners of weather and the scores of other games that you didn't want to watch. Advertising is more important than the actual game.

The greed factor in the sports arenas is a big part of the money race. When the focus is the money and not the exercise, the women and families suffer because the men are not getting the outlet for the energies that sports should provide.

Let's take back the sports for our families; take them back from the big business hustlers. With a fraction of the money spent on these sports-as-entertainment, we could provide modest facilities *in every community* that are free to the children, free to everyone—we all need the active participation for our mental and physical health.

Science

Science could obviously be used for the good of the human race and the planet, and most of the time it is.

A great amount of money is spent on science and everyone feels good about that—somehow it feels like you are giving to humanity when you give to science, so governments are happy to give to science and the scientists are happy, and the corporations who make millions on the products created by science are happy.

Unfortunately, industry is now funding most of the scientific research and that research is largely in their own interests, be it chemistry or physics or engineering or medical or agricultural. Almost all research done on university campuses is funded by the armed forces or by companies partnering with universities, with all the infrastructure, property and administration funded with public money. Most of this research has foreseeable applications for industry, and the universities need industry money because the government (in cooperation with industry) is forcing them to do so by cutting transfer payments to education, (a boy's club cooperative move). The results are obvious—research that does not necessarily improve the Real Standard of Living (RSL), but furthers the *competitive* advantage of industry.

Look at some of the important research that has been developed; some is valuable, some is simply self serving.

Viagara, for example, has been developed to keep men competitive sexually?!?!? There is no safe remedy for the hot flashes of menopause, however.

Great amounts of money are spent on space exploration, amounts out of all proportion to the value of such research. Manned space flights are not justified—except to men who like these sexy scientific pursuits and the huge single-sourced industries that gain huge profits by supporting them. We now have scientists—some very strange people—who are advocating manned flight to Mars. Millions and millions (echoes of Carl Sagan here) are being spent on some male sci-fi fantasies. If you or I talked about taking a few hundred or a few thousand or a few million people to flee to another planet when threatened by the destruction of a big meteor, we would risk being drugged as mentally ill. In remote regions of our planet, these men are actually spending huge amounts of money on prototypes that replicate such Mars' walks in preparation for this line of space development. Put them in shackles and save us from their delusions. We should forbid research on Mars until we have eliminated the common cold. As Dave Barry wrote in his *Complete Guide to Guys*, "Guys like a really pointless challenge."

Barry also wrote,

> "The real reason for the Space Shuttle is that it is one humongous and spectacularly gizmo-intensive item of hardware. Guys can tinker with it practically forever, and occasionally even get it to work, and use it to place other complex mechanical items into

orbit, where they almost immediately break, which provides a great excuse to send the Space Shuttle up *again*. It's Guy Heaven."

We have brilliant scientists finding connections between the human nervous system and the immune system, while at the same time we have politicians approving more money to build faster fighter jets. One B2 bomber costs $1B, and if the computer system fails, the plane is not flyable manually. There are 21 of these B2 bombers assigned to the 509th Bomb Wing of a US Air Force base.

So the scientists spend lots of money to try to save people's lives and a great deal more money to try to kill them.

Kim Vincente wrote in *the Human Factor: Revolutionizing the Way People Live with Technology* that medical error is the 8th leading cause of death in the US, the equivalent of a wide body jet airliner crashing every one or two days with no survivors. Science is subject not just to human error but the science may also be a cause of error.

Investigations into the oceans are truly a worthy pursuit, finding new life forms—not killing them. Investigations into the nature of insects and animals are vital to the understanding of our world and how we can live in it. Yes.
But, as in most male pursuits, science becomes a competition, a race to clone the first animal, to clone the first person, to be the first to the moon, to be the first first first. And as in everything men do, they lose sight of the reason for doing something when they get caught up in the competition, when the competition becomes the end purpose. Doing the first heart transplant and losing the life of the patient because the procedure was performed prematurely is typical.

Can't we let science serve the people and the planet as we would like to see technology do?

Education

Women have gradually staked their claim in higher education, but it has been a long time coming through the dark, darker and twilight years. But many years ago before the big regressions under male leadership, women were not less than men in the great classical schools of knowledge. Women were welcomed in the Pythagorean schools in 500 BC and in Plato's academy.

Unfortunately, though women are encouraged to get a higher education, the methods of teaching and testing are not well suited to female learning or to male learning either. These teaching methods, not surprisingly, have become big competitions. Sports are competitive because that is mostly what sports are all about. But education, under male leadership, also has to be a competition with deadlines and big winners—you must complete this course within 3 months and pass a brain-wrecking test or you can't learn anymore. And if you aren't rich, you have to compete for a scholarship before you can take the fast-frame courses.

The "tougher" courses virtually try to break the students down. Engineering and medicine come readily to mind. These elite students must prove themselves in the fires of academia or face the rest of their life being losers. It is all about pressure, not about learning and loving and using the knowledge.

Medicine has impossible demands—interns and residents work 36 hours at a time. What madness is this? Does anyone want a doctor treating them who hasn't had a break in 36 hours?

Engineers must take 6 courses a term, several with lengthy lab requirements, and one poor mark puts them at risk of losing their place in the faculty.

The whole driving concept seems to be that the degree is to be won through ordeal-by-university, eliminating the non-competitor who may be just as effective a doctor, engineer or lawyer as the ones who have honed their more aggressive *speed learning* skills. By rewarding the student who can fast track her or his learning skills, the society gains lots of doctors who can get the patients in and out of their offices the fastest and can take the most patients in a day. These are not necessarily the best doctors.

Lucille Ball was not good at script readings and would quite possibly never get a gig these days for that reason. But she would take a script home and make it her own like nobody else has ever done. She was not the fastest on the block but she was the best, yet we fail the student who can't "keep up".

The whole purpose of education in this male ivory tower is to get the reward—not necessarily to learn and understand anything. Students must spit out that 3 months of learning, (most of which has made little sense to them) in a 2 or 3 hour exam to get the reward in order to proceed to the next level—

UNLESS they have a learning disorder, (with a doctor's verification), in which case they can use a computer or whatever they need in a special facility, be invigilated by special staff, and can take as long as they need.

Now, almost all the students would do better if they had all the time they needed. They wouldn't choke under the time restraints, so their brains would function better. They would have the time to sort out their ideas and choose the most impressive responses.

My beef here is not that special needs students are getting university degrees when other worthy students may not be, because many of these learning disorder students are very intelligent, but why aren't *all* the students encouraged to actually learn things and then be asked to demonstrate that learning in a civilized manner, not just flex their cramming skills?

What do time limits have to do with learning?

Only in a male created education system does this style of education make male-logic sense. Get the students in and out of the institutions so the institution can take the tuition from the next group. Rational thinking would indicate that pressure and fear, deadlines, and time limits block a person's ability to think, and, consequently, work against the learning process.

Conversation

Conversation, for heaven's sake, is yet another competition with many men, (not all men). They are not able to discuss things or they can discuss things for a while, and then the exchange of ideas becomes a competition.

For example:

Matthew tells Joan that he thinks they need a fence on the sideyard. Actually, he has already decided that they need a fence.

Joan thinks about it.

"Depends, I guess, on what type of fence. What did you have in mind?" she asks.

"Just a regular wood fence, solid on the bottom and lattice on top," he says.

"Hmmm. Maybe we could try a fence like the one on Fernwood St. that has an open frame indented a foot or more every six to eight feet with climbing vines—looks good," Joan suggests.

"Ummmhmmm." She never agrees with any of his ideas. He expected this.

She goes on, "I think we should look at some possibilities before we commit to something we might not like."

"I like the fence idea. It would keep the dogs and the deer out, and they have the lumber cut already at the lumberyard. I could build it in a week," Matthew continues.

"Well don't you think we should look around at some other options?"

"You can if you like."

"How about a hedge?" she says. "Trees wouldn't be so harsh."

"You're saying you don't want an actual fence?"

"I really think we should be more creative—we have to live with it a long time." He never wants to discuss anything and it is frustrating.

"Okay, I *said* you can look at other ideas," he complains, "You don't have to get so intense."

"I am not getting intense", she says.

"Yes, you are."

"I'm trying to keep the options open."

"Well, they're your options. Keep them open."

"Don't you see? It is better to look at these ideas before we put out the money and then regret it."

"I don't want to argue about this, Joan."

"I'm *not* arguing."

"Well, you *sound* like you're arguing."

And the discussion deteriorates into an argument as Joan tries to explain what she means, and Matthew takes each effort as an escalating challenge for control.

Joan is frustrated wondering why the discussion can't be more productive, why they can't simply discuss the best thing to do like rational human beings. His purpose is to apprise her of the eminent fence-building project. Her purpose is to decide what would be the best solution for the sideyard. She ends up in or near tears, and she wonders why so many *discussions* end this way.

Matthew doesn't understand what is happening either. He just wanted to know if they should put up a fence *or not*. He is into the linear thing of we do this or we don't. He thinks she's being unreasonable and that she always wants her own way, wants to control everything, because whenever he makes a suggestion, she wants to change it. He has to resist her ideas because he perceives them to be a challenge. And the conversation becomes more and more a competition that he has to win. Then the competition overshadows the original purpose, which was whether to build a fence around the sideyard, and it is unfortunate if her feelings get hurt.

This kind of conversation can fall into the "verbal abuse" category when one person turns the exchange into an attack on the other. However, I think this particular exchange is largely the effect of the competitive male nature when a man feels he is being challenged for dominance whenever his ideas are challenged (which his ego identifies with his core personality) or when he perceives them to be challenged. He then has to win.

Invariably, communication between the Joans and the Matthews breaks down, and acrimony can replace an otherwise loving respectful relationship.

A conversation is not a contest. We don't have to have a winner and a loser. An unwillingness to toss your ideas around is the sign of a closed mind that is the special formula in which conflict breeds and fights arise—and wars develop. One friend of mine who is married to a lawyer complains that she gets cross-examined every time she opens her mouth. That is the farside of male conversation.

On the other hand, an architect I know runs every meeting in an enlightened forum of idea development. Everyone attending the meeting must contribute their viewpoints on the agenda items— they are expected to do their homework and come to the meeting prepared. No one is allowed to speak uninvited until everyone at the table has put forth their ideas. Then they are discussed. The meeting remains constructive and not competitive when every voice is given time and respect. This gives the quieter people, who often have wonderful ideas that are never heard, an opportunity to contribute.

This is the basis behind the native indian consensus decision-making also, a practice that we threw out in the European culture wash of North America. It is also the purpose behind the native "talking stick".

This inclination of men to turn a conversation into a competition where only the louder pushier voice (be it male or female) is heard is why we need to diminish male leadership, to guarantee the hearing of the wisest ideas, not the adversarial court system or team fight that pits ideas in the gladiator arena.

Competition = poor decision-making

A very dangerous job is King crab fishing in Alaska. There you would expect cooperation and mutual selflessness in the face of such shared hazards. One successful captain of a crab boat, however, stated that greed and competition are the biggest factors in the perils of the job. Refusing to pack it in when conditions clearly indicate they should, wanting just one more haul, wanting the pride of the biggest catch, are all widow-making decisions.

Fairer, healthier, family oriented, and wiser ideas and decisions are absolutely necessary to a world at risk, a world put at risk by the males in competition.

(6) MEN & WAR

Men and Explosions

Men blowing things up: boom, boom, boom.

You see these images in almost every movie promo ever put on the screen. Trains, planes, boats, cars and trucks; kaboom.

And men love these movies.

A strange phenomenon this is. It can hardly be instinctive since the Neanderthal surely didn't have explosives. Yet, many young boys have experimented with homemade bombs. One of my sons was involved in a Halloween bomb-making escapade, which I found alarming. Then I had some first year university male students write about their adolescent experiences. Approximately 15-20% admitted to fabricating something that exploded.

Is this some kind of male fantasy that hasn't a name? Certainly, Hollywood, that science lab of all things fantasy, knows about this craving for blowing stuff up. Many movies are now a series of explosions with no plot whatsoever.

Hot Wheels has a toy called *Beast Bash* that is all about shooting monsters, baring teeth and kill, kill, kill. Hot Wheels, for heaven's sake.

We can all take great delight in smashing things when we need to placate the gods of destruction. But this "explosion syndrome" is a riddle that I have found no sources of information on.

Obviously, however, if you take men's love of competition and combine it with the thrill of explosions, you are going to get WAR. And you get suicide bombers also, it seems. You get men (and a rare befuddled woman), who actually agree to blow themselves up, and they won't even get to enjoy the explosion.

Any way you look at it, there are many men designing bombing things and mining fields to blow people and vehicles up, and the others are watching shooting and killing in violent movies.

Following from the idea that the ultimate male high is killing, is it any wonder that all they need to hear is the trumpet call and they march behind Gideon wherever he leads because they will be given the ultimate male challenge—kill or be killed. (Gideon, of course, had God's support in his war efforts, though God did not tell Gideon to slaughter the Midianites in retreat. Nor did God tell him to take advantage of his glorious victory and bed a bunch of women.)

Hunting and fighting is what the male physique is designed for. That is why the male of the species is bigger, more agile, has better shoulder action and has better full body coordination as Dr. Richard Restak found in his studies of males and females. That is why the male is wylier, more aggressive, more single-minded, and usually more ruthless than women.

We can justify war as the necessary protection of our freedoms, to ward off the evils of evil groups. But now we have the Pentagon engaging in "preventative war" or "preemptive war". You really have to watch the euphemisms in war talk. Preventative war is simply one nation starting a war when no other nation has attacked that nation. By calling it "preventative war", however, they are able to forgive themselves for starting a war. And men who ran away from the risk of getting maimed in previous wars are now setting up the wars—to protect their countries. Any country is happy to wreak havoc on another country if they think the odds are strongly in their own favor, not thinking that they may be one of the *other* countries one day. Killing entails retaliation, which is more killing which again requires retaliation, which is more killing, and it never stops.

Previously, it was only the mad men, the Hitler's, the Stalins, the Pol Pots who started wars and killing in mass numbers. But now we have the good guys starting wars and killing hundreds of thousands of people.

As Riane Eisler wrote in the Chalice & the Blade (1987):

"Be it in the name of national defense . . . or in the holy name of God, . . . war or the preparation for war serve not only to reinforce male dominance and male violence, but . . . also . . . strong man leadership and also justify the suspension of civil liberties and rights"

As she writes, wars are directly linked to the need of males to dominate and all our societies are male dominant.

* * *

Yes, we have a new war—a War on Terrorism.

In April, 2002, the headline in British Columbia was "Probes begin amid sorrow," above this headline was a banner in black:

Killed in the line of duty: Sgt Marc Leger, Cpl Ainsworth Dyer, Pte. Richard Green, Pte. Nathan Smith.

Four young Canadian men in their 20s were killed in Afghanistan by a US fighter pilot who bombed them by mistake while on a training exercise (injuring 8 others). The picture in the paper shows Sgt Marc Leger's wife holding a picture of her husband posed in front of a Canadian flag wearing his combat uniform and his Princess Patricia Canadian Light Infantry beret.

Only a male world would celebrate these deaths as "killed in the line of duty" making this wanton stupidity appear to be an honorable situation.

And what is Canada doing on the ground fighting in Afghanistan is the first question that should be investigated, not the four investigations into the "friendly fire" deaths of four Canadian soldiers.

Canada has always been a peacekeeping country and these were the first Canadian soldiers killed in action in almost half a century,— killed in ground actions while the US were showboating their airborne might high above the kill zones. By June, 2007, there were over 50 Canadian soldiers killed in Afghanistan. Other than being told to by NATO and the US, we have no idea why we are there. Al Qaeda doesn't live there—the Taliban live there. Did the Taliban bomb the World Trade Center? I don't think so.

When asked why we went to war and provided the US air force with practice targets, Art Eggleton, Minister of National Defence in Canada, replied that we went to war in Afghanistan "to deploy an infantry battle group as part of a larger United States brigade to stabilize the region around Kandahar . . . The mission will speed the restoration of a legitimate government, remove risks to the people of the Kandahar region from mines and unexploded ordnance, and facilitate the delivery of humanitarian relief and the reconstruction of local infrastructure."

Apparently, we weren't there to defend our country or even any threat to our way of life. We were there to restore a stable government! That is a choker—what previous government in Afghanistan was stable?

He also seems to say here that the Canadian army was going to find all the land mines and rebuild the water, power and sewer systems alongside the Americans. We now have an army of plumbers and electricians? Eggleton didn't say a word about killing terrorists. Interesting how war motives take slippy slidey turns. If we are going to rescue every dysfunctional nation, we are going to be very busy. First we will be busy deciding which ones to save.

It is like cultural/religious proselytizing. The Afghan govt has control of Kabul and nowhere else, and they are happy to take our money, especially when all they have to do is say what a great job we are doing, and how things will be 'genocidal' if we leave. You have to use the genocidal word to get us to our knees. They don't say that they have no central government, that their tribal leaders and government leaders are suspected of keeping the country in chaos so that we will do the job they don't want to do. Also, with the Canadians pressuring the people who don't support the corruption of the government, the opium chiefs can continue to thrive building themselves what the Afghani call Opium Houses, mansions amid the poverty. They don't have the wherewithal to grow other crops, apparently.

Eggleton said that the House of Commons debated Canada's role twice, on Sept 25 and October 15, 2001, and voted in support of Canada's active participation in the "campaign". Those debates, the first one 2 weeks after the 9-11 bombings in New York and the second a month after, were held in the wake of the horrifying 9/11 murders, and the debates were not consequential to the decision.

Later, when people had time to reflect on the events and learn about the American history with the Taliban and Bin Laden, and the Saudi princes, and witness the bloody retaliation and revenge that was happening, many of the people were less enchanted with the actions taken. The US government was frantic for friends to support their actions, however, and Canada ran forward to join the Team. Our government did not want to be seen as anything but a good neighbor, and if killing is part of the friendship then we kill. Some coercion is always involved. We somehow managed to stay out of the Iraq war. Recently, there was a brief mention, (seen only once) that the mastermind behind the 9-11 attacks in New York was born in Kuwait. Wait a minute. Wasn't that the country George Bush Sr. went to war to protect in the war against Iraq?

Eggleton says that Canada cannot be neutral in the coalition campaign against international terrorism.

No one asks that we condone terrorism, but there is a huge difference between being actively opposed to terrorism and actively attacking a nation that is not fully responsible for the terrorism. Most of the 9/11 attackers were Saudi Arabians. The terrorists were trained in Pakistan. And a lot of money supporting Al Qaeda came from Saudi Arabia yet no one is planning to attack Saudi Arabia or Pakistan.

Incidentally, Mr Eggleton wrote his endorsement of the war at the same time that he received a 15 page report on military personnel behavior that he had hired a former girlfriend to prepare, for which the Canadian government paid $36,000. Ah, the dirt under the fingernails of these leaders.

The male world created the chaos, and then the male world tried to resolve it with more violence, and in both the creation and the destruction, the women and the families took a huge hit.

And 9 years later we were still there huntin' Taliban, or somebody.

And maybe the offensive in Afghanistan has liberated many of the people (who haven't been killed or aren't now starving in refugee camps in Pakistan), but you have to say that the need for this liberation would not have existed if the men in all these countries, Afghanistan, Russia, Pakistan, America etc. etc. had not taken on the killing missions in the first place.

There was an interesting statement in an Associated Press report by Nancy Benac titled "Americans Underestimate Iraqui Death Toll". About the attitude to the war, she stated that

> "Women are more likely than men to feel worried, compassionate, angry, and tired; men were more likely than women to feel proud."—a finding consistent with traditional differences of the sexes in attitudes toward war. For women, said [Christopher] Gelpi, (a Duke University political scientist) "there is an emotional response to casualties that men don't show . . . It could be some sort of socialization that men get about the military or combat as being honorable that women don't get.'"

"Ours is not to reason why, ours is but to do and die."

Beat the drum and the flock will follow: leaders call for support, the propaganda in the media increases (the movie *Top Gun* over and over, and rah-rah shows on the training of a pilot to fly the F16 American fighter planes) where the enemy becomes a hideous monster with little resemblance to a human being. And the atrocities are inevitable. We are aghast at the brutality of *the enemy* that we are shown—the crimes committed by the soldiers in war. Somebody's son disembowelling another person. Somebody's brother raping women in war. Somebody's father cutting the jewelry off a dead enemy.

Seamas Milne wrote in the London Guardian after Sept 11, 2001,

> "Bin Laden and his mojahedin were armed and trained by the CIA and MI6 as Afghanistan was turned into a wasteland and its communist leader Najibullah left hanging from a Kabul lamp post with his genitals stuffed in his mouth."

That was done by somebody's son. Would a mother ever believe her son could be capable of such an act?

We need to understand the nature of the male species.

The leaders do not even find out who the enemy is before they kill. In Afghanistan, the US handed out money to victims, and they also gave Afghans money to tell them where the Al Quaeda were, and because the Afghans wanted the money so badly, they named people and places not knowing if they were Al Quaeda or not. Apparently only 7% of the hundreds of prisoners in Abu Graib were arrested by the Americans; the others were ratted on by other Iraqis. Terrible transgressions occur under the guise of war.

I wrote a poem once on marching into war whenever our leaders tell us to, carrying guns to kill the other hired guns, ending the poem with the lines,

> Turn around
> Your leaders are behind you.

It will never change as long as men are calling the shots in this world, because when they hear the bugle call, they form up in lines, put on their uniforms, grab the baseball bat or the spear or the rifle and they march behind the leader man.

Now, however, there are nuclear weapons that can obliterate everything but the ants and cockroaches.

History was war

History used to be written by men, and they included only the activities of men and that was largely wars and atrocities (occasionally the Queens got some mention). But in ancient times, before history documented male exploits exclusively, there were thousands of years of better times—the garden of Eden years—that have come to us as myths. Then the nomads decided to take the spoils of the residents, which must have resulted in marauding raids. Success at this must have emboldened them and over many years, the nomads have continued to take over the residents with their terrifying brutality until today, we have almost every earthly society dominated by the brutish and/or crooked nomads and the residents have come to accept corrupt rule as the normal social order.

Well, it isn't.

Every time the brutes get the upper hand, the culture regresses which is why so many people react so strongly when the governments cut funding of necessities and cultural pursuits and increase spending on the military.

The barbarians are only interested in the thrill of pillaging and raping and killing, and this is what our men are doing in our society. Those that aren't actually doing the coveting, raping and killing are giving others the license to do this by their sins of omission, their "not getting involved" sanctioned support.

Going back to the ancient gods, we have Zeus, the king of the gods, being both good and evil. He was at times a symbol of divine justice and goodness, and at others, a licentious Achaean warlord, glorying in his powers and ruthlessness. In this instance man does resemble the god since the same man can be both just and good and a licentious warmonger.

Look at the great Ramses.

Ramses the Great in the 1200s BC was a Pharoah who ruled Egypt for 67 years. He got to be Pharoah because his family, starting with his grandfather, were military heroes who fought their way into power. The mighty did get the spoils. Around 1274BC, Ramses ll took an army north to take some of the lands from the Hittites. In the famous Battle of Kadesh, perhaps the largest chariot battle ever fought, the results were indecisive. He was outnumbered in his offensive against the Hittites in the Hittite territory, (was duped into thinking the Hittites had left the area) then found he was cut off from the main part of his troops, yet managed to survive. Ramses tried again a few times, sometimes making some gains only to lose them a year later. Finally, he negotiated a peace treaty with the Hittite leader, Muwatallil ll. He hadn't beaten the Hittites, but back in Egypt he related great stories of his victories to his people and to his neighboring states to keep them in awe of his wonders. He then built great monuments and statues to himself and made himself the glorious *and fearsome* leader, the King Rat who struck terror into any potential challengers. On this reputation he was in power for 66 years.

Mao Tse Tung may have been a student of the Pharoahs, because he made the Great March in 1934 leading his army against Chiang Kai Shek's nationalists for over a year. The march was actually a complete failure ending up with 20% of his army barely intact at the end of it. But Mao lied about the many defeats and the huge human cost and turned the fiasco into a winning platform that put him in power for many years after World War 2. He left extensive unmarked burial sites along his ignominious route to glory.

And in the 2000s, we had George W. Bush in a grinding failure of a war with deaths every day—a huge human slaughter—risking a third World War, and denying that the venture was a colossal failure. By lies and denial, was his administration hoping to parlay the failure into full control of the world? Given the compliance of the US government and judicial bodies, and the unworkable checks and balances on Presidential power in so-called wartime, we see the same old tactics used by the megalomaniacs without regard for the human sacrifices.

We need some studies on why people let this happen. Do they so badly want to believe their leaders aren't corrupt madmen that they have to deny the reality?

In a man's world, it is probably necessary to run around flaunting their military might. This is the language Al Quaeda and the other mighty leaders speak; they only respect brute force. So you can't lose credibility; you have to be seen to be very powerful or the whole deck of cards could crumble.

Ramses hardly had to do anything but popularize his legend and flaunt his wealth and power for the rest of his 66 years as Pharoah. He built his own statue the same size as the statues of the two most powerful gods thus making himself the equivalent of a god. The glory and the power was good for Ramses, but not so good for the Israelites whom he enslaved to build his two cities, Horeb and Ramses.

Men have ever rallied behind these daring hugely ambitious leaders. Many men were happy to go to war in World War 2. It looked like some of them just wanted to get out of the house, and it probably was, because when there is the call to the higher male performance, the men are eager to pit their skills against the adversary. Like kids who think they are immortal and race cars around town killing their friends, men don't think they will lose. Three million men fought in the Battle of Stalingrad in Russia in 1942; two million of them died. Two million sons, husbands, and siblings. Most of those that didn't die came back maimed or crippled and/or mentally damaged.

The father of one of my friends returned to Vienna from the Russian front after WW2. He was unrecognizable to his wife, barely spoke the rest of his life, and drank continuously for the remaining 25 years of his life. Over and over, those damaged "defenders" return to create dysfunctional families, who then proceed to propagate more dysfunctional families for generations.

And the US felt justified in killing a hundred thousand Iraqis (and 4500 Americans military) to avenge the deaths of approximately 3500 US citizens in New York knowing full well the Iraqis had not been behind the 9/11 deaths.

Unfortunately, the killing doesn't stop when the armistice is declared and all the game's players congratulate themselves for a game well played, and the movies cash in on the pathos. The mines and mortar from the two world wars are still killing people. In 1991, there were 36 French farmers killed by mortar and mines struck by their farming machines in the fields. A farmer finds an average of 10 fragments of bombs and mortar per summer.

There is a whole squad of men in Europe, deminers they are called, whose job is to clear land of killing armaments. In a square meter, the deminers have found up to **2 tons** of killing stuff. They are even finding chemical weapons in canisters from WW1 that are badly rusting, the casings leaking gas that fills the lungs and drowns the victim. This squad is working fulltime, but they estimate at the rate they are clearing areas, it will take 700 years before all of France will be clear and safe. 700 years before the killing from the 1ˢᵗ and 2ⁿᵈ world wars will be over. That's a lot of killing going on.

Think about the honor in killing the farmer that feeds us.

The land mine story is interesting.

In 1992, Senator Leahy got a bill through the US Senate to place a moratorium on antipersonnel landmines for a year. In 1993, he had an amendment to extend the moratorium for one year. In January 1996, Canada agreed to support such a move. There were an estimated **100 million unexploded landmines in over 60 countries in the world** that kill an estimated 26,000 civilian people each year. Some of these landmines are designed to maim not kill, to blast off the victim's legs to the knees as a terrifying deterrent to other soldiers. The "bouncing betty" landmine is designed to "pop up" to waist height and shatter everything in a 360° radius. So who is building these landmines? Many of the Cambodian landmines were made in China, and the intelligent computer chip inside the landmine is made by Motorola. Princess Diana was actively campaigning against the horrors of the landmines before she was killed in the car accident in Paris.

The makers of these weapons are killing us all, the allies and the enemies. The landmines are only a part of the "conventional weaponry" us peace-loving nations are selling. If there are 100 million unexploded landmines in the world, think about how much money someone made manufacturing those landmines.

What is war doing to people?

Watching movies of previous wars, watching the brave men standing tall for their country, the depiction of the heroics of the defenders of our way of life, we can't help but be proud. Recently, on a radio request program near Armistice Day, there were several of the old feel-good-about-war songs requested: It's a Long Way to Tipperary, Pack up Your Troubles in Your Old Kit Bag, and We'll Meet Again. There is an irresistible thrill to these depictions of the human spirit facing the greatest challenge that seems to come from way down inside the reptilian psyche in all of us. We visualize an image of the soldiers so brave, so valorous, so attractive in their clean uniforms, even when we know that the reality of that *Meeting Again* will be when he is crippled and broken, his uniform bloody and smelling of burnt human entrails.

The reality outside the glorious songs and movies is hideous and horrible, and it's gotta stop.

One of my insightful first year university students wrote in an essay on irony:

> "Until we stop investing our time and money in killing and start investing it in helping others, it is an ironic statement to call the human race intelligent." Josh Brand

The human race is intelligent until the hormones (testosterone) and the endorphins surge past the logic, and then the human being becomes a killing machine without any human attributes.

Men seem to be addicted to war just as gamblers are addicted to gambling. The money or the cause becomes irrelevant as they succumb to the rush of the risks and dress up in their special clothes—fancy clothes, if possible, but fatigues will do.

Recently, I was struck by some pictures taken of German officers at Auschwitz in 1945 who were wearing incredible uniforms and magnificent hats. This picture was taken in 1945 when their whole nation was starving and they were killing millions in their Final Solution—they still had the money for the splendid uniforms to feed their fantasies of superiority.

Women could provide the necessary checks and balances, but the fact is, that when an international crisis develops, (which men create) suddenly women disappear.

When there is talk of war, when the bad guys threaten our freedoms, our democracy or our way of life, suddenly men are featured in every news-breaking mode, interviewing, analyzing, reporting, presenting options—options within the framework of war, of course. Brilliant men—they are brilliant men—but they are brilliant within the parameters of the male response. And the brilliant women become simply incidental providers for the needs of the warriors. After Sept 11, we only saw men everywhere on TV as the male hormones surged and the chests puffed up, and they prepared for the big fight challenge, talk, talk, talk, bomb, bomb, bomb.

Now we are capable of serious mass destruction, and with this power to destroy the whole world in a nuclear war, men actually consider using nuclear weapons and talk about the odds of survival—*the odds of survival*. They are willing to put the survival of the human race up like a crap shoot.

The Bush administration has set aside the disarmament pacts that were in place. The American government wants to disarm every country in the world except their own, because somehow they believe that they should have the right to weapons of mass destruction and no one else should. Nothing in US history leads us to think that the Americans are less gunhappy, less killing-oriented, less violent, less corrupt than anyone else. To the contrary. We have already seen how too much power has turned the American leaders into world bullies where might is always right. At this very moment, they are roaming the world looking for someone to beat up. Mitt Romney, the aspiring GOP presidential candidate said in a speech, that, as President, he would build the mightiest military on earth.

When Russian Premier Putin put a damper on the US plans to target Iraq, (May 24, 2002) the next day we heard that southeast Asia would be a possible target. They hit Iraq with Shock & Awe anyway.

They are always in the market for a new enemy should they need one to justify their military spending.

Andrei Illarionov, a prominent liberal economist in Russia, who once worked under Putin, was quoted saying,

> "Putin reacts traditionally. If they have no real enemies, they create them. They need enemies. They cannot live without enemies. If all enemies are destroyed, then there is Yaboko, the Republican Party, the Right Forces, the Other Russia—they'll finish these enemies. It's a natural law of dictatorship."

And it is a natural law of pseudo dictatorships as well—keep an enemy handy.

Well the world can't survive with this attitude by those controlling the money in the world. Pakistan and India and China have nuclear weapons. Indeed, the Slumbering Giant, China, is waking up and has built an underground submarine and warship base near Sanya in Southern Hainan Island as part of its effort to challenge the American naval presence in Southeast Asia. The ships are nuclear ballistic missile submarines that have a firing range of 8000 miles—ie. can reach 4/5ths of North America if fired just off the coast of China. In response to China's Sanya base, India is ramping up their war machine and building a similar naval base, and we are now facing a whole new version of the weapon's race.

The world simply can't survive.

As long as men run the world, we will always have war—we will always have the hideous deaths, the broken lives, the maimed bodies, the end of fruitful pursuits. The US Senator McCain, when seeking the Republican nomination in 2008 for the Presidency, talked about a "presence" in Iraq for a 100 years—the conquerors would *stay the course*. He was a POW in Vietnam who was tortured and yet he was very much in favor of war, and he is very much in favor of US imperialism, which is an ideology that factors in violent control. Is this not madness? McCain protested the Democratic interest in renegotiating NAFTA because he thinks it would jeopardize the US control on the Canadian military. As he said, "We need the Canadian military." The trade deal is only a factor to him in as much as it pertains to war and hegemony. The US compromised our autonomy (& sovereignty) in NAFTA and NATO and we are fighting in Afghanistan as a result. Afghanistan is controlled by thugs—and as long as the Afghan thugs kill Canadians regularly and blow things up, they will continue to make headlines in our papers and we will continue to send them money.

Newt Gingrich, in a speech when campaigning for the Republican nomination on January 17, 2012, stated loudly, "Like Jefferson, when asked what to do with the enemy, *we will kill them.*" The whole crowd cheered wildly. What enemy? They really want enemies.

Living in this male dominant insane asylum with governments spouting Jesus and Mohammed values and wrapping that around F16s bombing children and women (and all others) in impoverished countries is absolute madness—surely we will all become unhinged, if we aren't already, and Prozac is not the answer.

It is time for these deadly war games to end. The huge sacrifice of human life, usually of those at the peak of their young lives who end up being missile fodder, and the waste of huge amounts of money that could be used to improve lives and the planet our lives depend on must stop. If you visit the WW2 graveyards in Scotland, England or France, and you read the gravestones, you will find most of the dead were teen-agers, maybe one in 200 was 30years old. Why aren't the older men making the world safe for these young people?

But no, we are still raising our children to be martyrs to horrible people's ambitions, to die for reasons they don't even understand. Fifty thousand American soldiers died in Vietnam, [not counting the 300,000 Vietnamese], which means that more than 50,000 western families were torn apart with grief. On a plane on the runway at the San Francisco airport during the Vietnam War, my husband watched as workers unloaded a plane-load of bodies in body-bags from Vietnam. Why? The Socialist Republic of Vietnam's economic growth is now among the highest in the world since 2000. What was gained? Unfortunately, their market-economy reforms have also caused a rise in income inequality and gender disparities. (Wikipedia, 2012)

Bill Moyers commented

> ". . . You try to . . . discount the thrill of war for those who advocate it but never have to suffer from it."

That says a great deal about what we are talking about in this book.

Is war really necessary to satisfy the male needs to defy the odds, to gain stature, to be glorious? Aren't there other ways that men can achieve these rewards?

I think there is. Look what we find now in these reality TV challenge shows. We get the same thrill, the same breath-holding excitement from watching teams of men and women pit themselves against the other teams, against the fates and the natural forces as we do from watching the war shows. We can marvel at the amazing resilience, perseverance, organization, strategy, strength and spirit that it takes in Mark Burnett's TV series, *Eco-challenge*. Or we marvel at regular people facing their fears on *Fear Factor*, and *No Opportunity Wasted*, and the *Amazing Race*, with boggling fearless spirit, and no one has to be killed to give us this human example of people facing their fears and defying the odds. And the women are as successful as the men, yet the challenges are no less demanding.

Men don't need war in the 21ˢᵗ Century.

It's gotta stop.

(7) MEN & SOCIAL CONTROL

The deregulated western reverence for the individual above the common good is killing us. It gives men the right to cheat each other, destroy each other with unfair competition for their own individual gain. It is the 80s all the time, the big "me" generation that never ends.

Dr. Dean Ornish said it so well,

> "An individual does not exist in isolation from everyone and everything else, but exists in the context of a community, family, workplace, religion and so on."

Men definitely choose the better social role than women. For example, I worked for a year in a government office as an executive secretary on an executive floor. The secretaries and clerks came to work at 8:15 (precisely 8:15) and left at 4:30. Once at work, we lesser creatures were tied to the phones. If we went to the copier or the printer stations we forwarded our phones so that no calls would be missed. Now, I suppose, it is better as you could forward your phone to a cell phone and go to the pub if you chose. But not 20 years ago. Yet the executives were free to breeze in and out on their way to meetings—ahhhh, meetings—and the straight jacket of the compulsory imposition on their time was much less stressful.

If men don't have the better role they soon change the roles/rules to get the better role.

I realized that having time constraints imposed on your day—that are not of your choosing—is quite possibly the most stressful aspect of life, be it your work life or your home life. Little tots going to daycare everyday at 8 in the morning—getting up, having breakfast, getting into their coats and then getting strapped into the car seat can't be a good thing. Yet that is the structure this male society has imposed on all the citizens. And if you can't function in this framework, you are a failure, a loser.

I have seen cashiers in big box Depot chains that are multitasking for 8+ hours at a frenetic pace with phones ringing, music blaring, and they themselves making PA announcements and calling supervisors, all while ringing through purchases. How do they do it?

The first nations people can rarely adhere to these arbitrary work times, which simply demonstrates they have a much saner grip on human realities. I couldn't do it. After a year, I quit the 8:15-4:30 job. Maybe if that is the only job you have ever had, you find a way to stay in it; I really don't know. But we expect people to do these jobs year after year and in the US many of those jobs provide one week holiday a year.

The hunter-gatherer spent about 4 hours a day providing for their food, getting exercise, fresh air, and stimulating challenges at the same time. The lion on the savannah works about 2 hours a day and then lies in the grass. No animal, except those we have domesticated with force, will constrain its activities to these psyche-damaging time constraints.

It is not only our day-to-day personal work demands that are controlled beyond what humans are designed to do, but the bigger social mores are also constructed around controlling the behavior of others.

Our politics and even our religions are designed to justify the oppression of the many by the individual few.

Politics

Politics is the science of government; government being a body of persons authorized to administer the laws, or to govern a state.

It is also a position of power in which one group of persons makes the rules and then has the power to enforce the rules, a position remarkably suited to the needs of the control seekers and the status seekers.

For men of the ruling class—as we see over and over in our governments—justice and law are simply useful mechanisms to gain the power to take what they want and do what they want. They are in positions to manipulate the polling district boundaries, the voting lists, the polls, and even the actual voting mechanisms that can compromise an election to ensure certain outcomes.

There is currently a big upsurge in the competitive nature of the market economy, a particularly ruthless form of capitalism that ensures that only the strongest, the richest and the most ruthless will survive. This is not new, of course. Andre Gide was making similar observations in France in 1927 when he decried the abuses of the concessionary French companies in Africa that were exploiting African natives.

But now we all seem to be caught up in this money race where there is no room for the slowpoke, for those who don't have the dominant alpha male hormone activity necessary in this type of society. It is a known fact that most of the highest achievers have the highest levels of testosterone. Should it then be a surprise that men like Presidents Kennedy and Clinton were womanizing men with tremendous sex appeal? One woman claimed that when she was in the same room with former President Clinton, his charisma was "almost unbearable".

Politics, to most men, is really the art of wielding power, not about running a good government. These men in our governments often started out intending to "serve the people", to do a better job for the people than the previous government, but this soon becomes a hideously hollow joke. They all follow each other by taking and holding the line the man up the alpha ladder directs them to take. They will cosy up to any ruthless company or group if there is enough money in the pot to get them reelected.

Prime Minister Jean Chretien campaigned in Canada on the promise to rescind the GST which was a copy of Margaret Thatcher's VAT that never happened. He even made noises about getting out of NAFTA, but later as the Prime Minister, he actively campaigned other countries to sign on to the even bigger trade agreement, the Trade Agreement of the Americas.

When the Free Trade Agreement was being negotiated between the US and Canada (the forerunner to NAFTA), the US trade team set a date for Canada to sign up for the agreement. The day came and the Canadian negotiators said Canada couldn't sign: there were too many concessions against Canada and none on the US side. But to "save face" with the big American trade dogs, Brian Mulroney, Prime Minister at the time, flew to Washington that night and signed the agreement for which he was given a state dinner in Washington. He had not even read the document. Apparently, no Member of Parliament had actually read the book-length document—they didn't have time to read it before the deadline. Mulroney has since been the most hated Prime Minister ever elected in Canada. NAFTA was not about leveling the playing field for the signees, it was about giving the corporations a free ride in international opportunities. As seen in the subsequent softwood dispute between Canada and the US, there was no intention of actually having fair trade.

But what about the deadline thing, the time constraints on decision-making? The trade negotiators are all about deadlines, and deadlines are all about winning the race. If they don't set deadlines, men won't know if they have won. They won't get the blue ribbon for first.

What is there to gain from these deadlines?

Deadlines are very anti-human unless they are deadlines to end war.

The First Nations' people have a school in Kelowna, BC, in which they teach the principle of Enow'kin, which is a consensus type of decision making. The idea is to understand the opposing opinions—to put yourself in their mental shoes until you see their point of view. Present your position, discuss, and then arrive at consensus—not a 51% majority. They believe that a 51% majority decision leaves 49% unhappy with the decision, and these 49% will probably have to be forced to cooperate—this is not effective for the long term or the short term because those 49%ers may grow to be 51%ers who want revenge.

If the First Nation's group does not meet with a consensus agreement, they shelve the issue and they carry on without a resolution. They carried on before the pow-wow on the issue, and they do so again. Surely this is an enlightened means to resolve issues.

(Unfortunately, not all First Nation's tribes are so enlightened and are subjected to much abuse at the hands of greedy tribal leaders as well—without recourse to as much justice as we are.)

What purpose do these arbitrary deadlines serve?

"If you don't hand over the hostages by Friday at 10am—we go to war. If you don't tell us what we want to hear, we bomb the hell out of you. If you don't sign this agreement by midnight, we won't invite you to our trade party, and you will SUFFER." Is this the behavior of grown-up people?

Why do we all accept these arbitrary rules made up by some self-serving King Rat playing his power game?

Deadlines are just that—DEADlines.

NAFTA, speaking of NAFTA, we find that the agreement has not been particularly good for the US people either. Northern Mexico has gained about one million new jobs since the signing of NAFTA which is good for Northern Mexico, not to mention India and Indonesia and many other cheap countries that gained significantly. All those Northern Mexico jobs, however, came from the US and Canada when the US companies moved their operations to Mexico to take advantage of the low wages and nearly non-existent environmental protections. The Agreement was also not good for the Southern Mexicans who are currently impoverished (estimates of 40 million Mexicans are impoverished) partly due to the increased living standard of the employed northern Mexicans.

So who wins with this NAFTA agreement?

Not many of the U.S., Canadian or Mexican people. Yes, okay, there are benefits for manufacturers and some others, but largely there are more downsides for the people and the environment. We had free trade in Canada since the fur trade, which was actually *freer* trade than the trade we now have with books filled full of restrictions about who we can trade with, and penalties fashioned in legalese that can be interpreted to suit those it serves.

For example, the ability to determine what is good for people in any one area has been taken away. If Canada or California decides that a fuel additive (MMT or MTBE) is making their people sick (and they are making people sick), these governments are not allowed to have these additives banned because that is a violation of the additive's companies' rights to do business as guaranteed by NAFTA.

Free trade actually handcuffs the governments, which is the ONLY purpose of these agreements, because corporations and power groups seem to be able to break these agreements whenever it suits them and no one stops them.

The disempowered governments have lost their ability to govern, to legislate in the interests of the people they govern, and they are all parroting the market-driven slogans like puppets on strings,

- o "leaner and meaner governments"—which means cutting all social programs that affect the low income people.
- o "there is no scientific basis to continue the moratorium on offshore drilling" BC, May 2, 2002—which means the government has been bought off with money or threats by the oil industry.
- o "government is being responsive to the public"—which means the government will be doing whatever the business councils recommend since the only public they talk to are business leaders.
- o "we need perimeter security around North America"—means the US will dictate the terms of immigration policy and "free" movement of the citizens of the US and of Canada and of Mexico.
- o "we will cut the burden of excessive government bureaucracies" means more deregulation which means there will be much less control of the princes of darkness in their greedy activities.

This abdication of government control over the decision making process in favor of big business has happened in successive moves.

For example, in Canada 20 years ago, we got the new "Charter of Rights" which gives individuals more rights of various kinds—in line with the US model. But what also happened with this Charter is that the rights of the society in which individuals live are taken away; government is less effective. And since none of us is an island unto ourselves, this Charter actually works against us individually by removing the protection of a person's group needs,—health care, security, fair laws etc. It also took away most of the powers of our elected members of government who have been rendered invisible in any decision-making function in our pretend democracy.

In May, 2001, a dozen countries, including Canada, sued some tobacco companies on money laundering charges, but the US government says those countries do not have the right to sue US companies. Under NAFTA, of course, the *companies can sue countries* and do so. Four months later, in the wake of the 9-11 distractions, the suit against the tobacco companies was dismissed.

So, by deregulating all the industries—letting them regulate themselves (if they choose to do so) and by "strengthening the rights of the individual" (the Charter of Rights)—and by the subsequent trade agreements, any governments' ability to govern has been weakened. And who gains?

Well, with a government handcuffed on the floor of the House, the robber barons can go ahead and loot the country, which they are doing progressively with the euphemistic free trade agreements, which give them the freedom to loot the country without being accountable to any government, especially in the financial markets. They are only accountable to their own tribunals that they themselves set up.

In the wild east, the bullies are more overt, as when the Chinese overran the Tibetans in 1959, a people who seemed to be fairly happy. But the Chinese warlords saw wealth they could pillage so they pillaged, raped, and murdered decent people by the thousands. They have moved many Chinese into the country to effect a cultural change from Tibetan to a majority Chinese.

Curiously, many of those Chinese who are now living in Tibet are choosing to embrace the mores of the Tibetans.

And here in the wild west, the bullies are less visible as they meet behind closed doors, where might is right and men are men and the gun still settles disputes.

Where is Robin Hood when you need him?

The Gross Domestic Product—the GDP

What is politics without mention of the Gross National Product or the Gross Domestic Product—the GDP? The GDP is the value of all goods and services produced by a country. It is used as an indicator of the health of a country's economy, a measure of who is winning in the economic race. If a government leader puts money toward the needs of the people, then that country can't play in the big leagues, and will lose its franchise, and will have to pay penalties by punishing their citizens. It's a rough league. What we need is a measure of our Real Standard of Living,—RSL—that takes into account how many people in a country per capita live below the poverty line, how many people are on antidepressants because their lives are unlivable, how many people are working at jobs they hate . . .

As the President of Malaysia said ". . . there is no longer anyone constraining capital, so capitalism no longer needs to be nice."

Justice

Justice and the law are also forums for competition, simply another arena for men to test their competitive skills. They set up the rules for justice and the biggest guns win. The innocence or the guilt of the person on trial is irrelevant as we saw in the OJ Simpson media circus where it was all tricks and cunning. Lawyers square off and everybody loses, usually huge amounts of money. Johnnie Cochrane Jr stated that when he went into his Assistant District Attorney's job in Los Angeles he was hoping to use the law to make society better, yet he later stated that "we can be friends, but once we get in that courtroom, we won't be friends." That isn't making society better.

The justice system is not only a big boys' competition, it is also another commercial opportunity. Those with the money—the lawyers, and the wealthy—can buy justice in today's system, and can bend the rules to favor the insiders.

I recently contested the terms of an estate. If I wanted to go to court, it would cost me about $100,000 plus lawyer's fees and other fees. And there was no guarantee that I would win, "You never know how a ruling will go when you go to court—anything can happen." If I lost, then I would be getting less than if I didn't go to court—even when I was plainly in the right and *everyone* involved admitted this.

Another time, I submitted a complaint about a lawyer to the BC Law Society that has a complaint process. One complaint I made was that the lawyer lied and cheated, and I had his own written statements showing the lie, which the Law Society reviewer dismissed. Another complaint I made that he threatened to continue his onerous charges if we didn't sign off his accounts, and I had his written statements showing the threat, the reviewer dismissed. When the offending lawyer was asked for financial statements, he simply didn't comply, yet this was also dismissable as being outside the limits of the complaint process. And I made other demonstrable allegations, but the *only one* the reviewer would acknowledge was my statement that he was rude, and I had no written proof of the rudeness, which he denied, of course. Surely, this was a case of the Society looking after their own and not functioning to resolve improper behavior. *There was no recourse against this lawyer.*

In the Vancouver Sun, April 25, 2008, we read the following:

> "A peculiar tick of the South Korean legal system is that judges, not wanting to upset the economic apple cart, rarely sentence corporate titans to long prison terms and seldom strip them of their empires. A recent study of white-collar prosecutions found that in 82 per cent of cases, South Korean judges released convicted executives without requiring prison time."

Often the cases go on for years, both criminal cases and civil cases and some divorce cases while people suffer psychologically and financially. Most of the time, the experience ruins their lives. One lawyer I know well tells me that when a divorce goes to court, nobody wins. She went into mediation with much more success.

This is not a good system as anyone will tell you who has tried to get justice in our court system. It seems the law faculties have unwittingly devolved into the business of teaching lawyers how to steal and cheat legally. It is all about the legal system and not much about justice.

Is the French system fairer? Some say no and some say yes. I hope to never find out. I have worked out a system that I think would be more fair but I am not convinced about the possible outcomes, corruption being what it is. I do believe the justice system should be about the parties involved in the dispute and not about the lawyers. The law should be simple enough for an accused person to understand and defend himself just as the tax system should be simple enough for the person paying the taxes to figure out.

Religion

St John of the Cross, a brilliant and devout Christian Carmelite monk in 16th Century Spain, described his "dark night of the soul" in which he had doubts of faith. This is explained in Catholic theology as a testing by god where the pious believer goes through a "stage" of their spiritual development when he or she feels abandoned by god. If the person remains faithful during the dark night of his/her soul, they will have come through the ordeal of his mettle-testing and will be exalted in the eyes of god. But St. John really didn't find his faith again. In fact, I believe St John recognized the big lies, that man does not have dominion over god's creation, and, more importantly, that there is no tangible god-person somewhere in the heavens who loving his children would suffer them to endure the agonies of terrible illnesses, would deny procreation by demanding celibacy of his priests, would deny the full rights of the mothers of god's children, would sanctify the killing of others in his name— this was the time of the Inquisition in Spain—or would give men permission to kill in his name or to mistreat animals, etc.

But when St John had invested all of his life in the Big Lie with considerable energy and much success—he became a true leader in the church—how could he deny everything when his whole world believed the Lie with such terrible consequences for those who didn't. When St John tried to introduce some reforms in the ecclesiastical system, other monks were directed to put him in prison, which they did. Later, of course, after he died, he was beatified as a saint, a strange reversal and another instance of god's law being formulated and interpreted to suit the guardians of the law. The inquisition served up a very compliant country of servants.

We had a similar example in the movie, "The Catholic" about an Irish abbot in a monastery who could no longer pray. His faith was truly being tested—*or put to the lie*. These are dramatic heart-breaking stories of real men facing the Big Lie with great courage.

But the Lie serves men over and over in their twisted efforts for domination, for power. The Crusaders went on Holy Crusades across Europe reaping the spoils as marauding nomads, all under the umbrella of god's work, believing themselves justified in male supremacy and forcing their beliefs on others.

The Salem witch-hunts tortured and killed women who refused to accept the Lie, another crime little men enforced with god as their witness.

Jesus never uttered a word about celibacy, and it would appear that the apostles themselves were normal married men, as Jesus probably was himself. In those days, every Jewish male was pressured to marry by the age of 21. Jesus did not deny women the preaching role. However, the writers of the Bible were men living centuries after Jesus lived, and their interpretations are male-purposed. And those male interpretations have added to the enslavement of women in Christianity just as the Muslim interpreters of the Koran have enslaved the women in their society. The Muslim men have terrified their women to such impossible lengths that women must hide in burkas, must not be seen. Many of these women now accept this oppression as a normal condition of a proper society.

Jesus had women in his apostolate according to the Gnostic gospels that predate the New Testament closer to the lifetime of Jesus (50-100ce).

Men have always used religion, whenever it was convenient to do so, to keep the masses subjugated. Having god back up your demands and your actions with the promise of eternal happiness for following their commands or eternal pain for not following their lead is a big motivator. Walking with god as your witness into war gives the whole killing thing real status. These war-mongering leaders actually assert that they are god-loving men in the same breath that they advocate killing. George Bush claimed to have walked around the White House grounds praying for guidance from god before invading Iraq. Did god tell him to get over there and bomb huge numbers of people?

And most of the wars are pinned on the right to practice one sect's religious freedom.

How hypocritical—Jesus was all about loving one's fellow man and turning the other cheek.

Does the Koran advocate intolerance and killing?

Why would a god create all things and then ask man to kill them?

In the 3ʳᵈ century, the Christian male church leaders took the direction of the Christian religion into their own hands, but before this overthrow by the men, women took turns leading the meetings much like the Quaker church today. Spiritual equality to Jesus meant including pagans in their services as well. There is evidence that some of the early Christians prayed to both Father and Mother. Some described the holy spirit as feminine so that the god in the three persons was father, mother, and son, certainly a more reasonable interpretation than the strange triad of Father, Son and Holy Ghost. (If man was made in the image of god, and god was (is) a trinity, then man must be all three, father, son and holy ghost. This is difficult.)

When the early male church leaders embraced the Paulist view they took the opportunity to selectively choose their texts to subvert women, and women who continued to participate as full teaching preaching members were branded heretics. Who we worship provides a strong structure for the modeling of society and if the feminine is excluded, then the female role is undervalued. But if we must set up human-like gods to worship, better that they reflect the whole miracle of procreation.

Jesus defended women and consorted freely with women, which was not acceptable at the time and may have been a large factor in his persecution and death at the behest of the Pharisees and Hebrew priesthood. (Certainly, championing the rights of women must have also led to the persecution of Socrates hundreds of years before Christ.)

The understanding that Jesus had of women and the role they played in his life appeals to many women. How these women reconcile the misogynistic direction of most religions with the love that Jesus had for the women and children is not clear to me.

I had much personal experience with the lack of value for women's roles in my life. When I was asked what I was going to do after grade 12, I said I would go to university. My father commented—"What does a girl need an education for?" He took his cue from the church that he relied on completely to define the values in his life. He believed Pope Paul V1 who said in 1977 that women were barred from the priesthood because "our Lord was a man". I don't think he ever forgave me for not knowing "my place".

Jesus taught compassion, nonviolence and love in contrast to some of the most powerful Christian and Muslim and Jewish leaders who advocate denial of female rights, revenge, terrorism and killing. There is no connection between the prophets and the practice of these religions.

Riane Eisler noted that in the Christian religion as interpreted by men, "Knowledge is bad, birth is dirty, death is holy". I have seen death and it didn't look holy, but this twisted anti-life stance has given men power for thousands of years, and none of the church leaders question the purpose of such a creed because the purpose serves their own interests.

In the Old Testament, we are told god approved of women's sexual slavery to men, and who does that serve?

In many Catholic areas in the Southern countries, the religion is curiously different than the Catholicism celebrated in the northern countries. In Las Vasquez, as in many other South American locations, the local natives have an annual pilgrimage to the Blessed Mother. They revere the Blessed Virgin, praying to her for her help and forgiveness, often crawling on their knees. They may have accepted the religion of the conquerors with the priests saying the mass and adoring Jesus, but they never stopped praying to the Mother.

We would do well to require all citizens and immigrants to sign a freedom waiver for their families that ensures each citizen has a right to choose his or her religion upon reaching the age of 16 without undue coercion.

Any society uncontaminated with the big lie recognizes that the Mother is foremost in the world making sure they get fed, and whose female connections ensure continued love, care, and upbringing.

- o It is the mom that stands between an enraged or abusive male and her children,
- o It is usually the mom who gets the food and prepares it,
- o It is usually the mom that nurses her children through short and long illnesses,
- o It is the Afghan women in Pakistan refugee camps who are starving themselves so that their children will survive, while the Taliban, the Northern Alliance, the British, the

American and the Canadian mighty men threaten their ability to live if they don't actually kill them.

o It is the young Islamic women who are speaking against the Islam radicals and the Islamic intolerances in Europe. Not the men, not the governments, not the older women who should be doing this for their daughters, it is the young women taking it on.

Christians are taught that we are all the children of God the father. No mother? We didn't get half our genes from our mother and half from our father?

One remarkable rebuttal to the Christian argument that women are not as worthy as men in the eyes of god was made by Sojourner Truth, an enslaved American black woman who achieved her freedom and went on to advocate for black and female rights. In Ohio, in 1851, when confronted with the argument that women were less than men because Jesus was a man and his 12 apostles were all men, she stood up in front of a large meeting and said,

"And where did your Jesus come from? He came from god and a woman; no man had anything to do with it."

(8) MEN & TECHNOLOGY

Technology is the blessing that truly liberates most of us from active physical labor, a true triumph in the pursuit of more comfortable lives.

But, alas, there are the consequences that go with any and all innovations and changes. From the wonders of nuclear energy, we became victims of the fear of nuclear weapons. In our fervor for the Easy Life, the computer age is probably killing us as effectively as the tigers and the wolves ever did. The computer age was supposed to give us extensive time off in which we would recreate ourselves in sporty lifestyles. The feature in every magazine 30-40 years ago was how we would fill in our time when we would only be working at our jobs for 4 hours a day. This, of course, never happened. Instead, the blue collar worker disappeared and the computer programmers who did get jobs were exploited 12 to 15 hours a day in cube farms. Burning out 32 year old workers in these new age jobs doesn't much matter to management because there are plenty more 22 year olds ready to take their places.

This technology also turns out to be a race, a competition in which the other team must be destroyed so that the winners have all the market share.

IBM, a pioneering company in computers, had a significant edge in the industry and then, as others like Compaq got into the market, they were pressured into publicly announcing new innovations and features before they were even fully developed. They started marketing to the educational institutions, promising delivery by a certain deadline, and then were unable to deliver. This jeopardized their whole operation what with the financial complexities involved. The world wouldn't have stopped if they didn't meet their own arbitrary deadlines, and the world didn't stop. In fact, who would really have given the proverbial "rat's ass" if they didn't even have a deadline. (The iPod comes to mind.) Again, the spirit of the competition, the male idea of win or lose, and all is lost if we lose mentality goes on and on.

Cars are a big technology gobbler, newer better models that are just newer different models with little better about them in the last 60 years. There have been nominal changes every year to appeal to the gadget-minded males, and the manufacturers have been forced to improve the safety of the vehicles, but they are still killing machines, killing machines that could be made safer and more environmentally friendly except they wouldn't be as sexy. But what is sexy is one of the innovations on a new high end American model—a car with a shower. Yep.

Another model has a feature that if you lock yourself out of the car, by calling a number you can get the car unlocked by satellite. And the vans have TV and DVD players to play movies for your children. Do they have to watch movies even in the car? What about the scenes they are driving past?

Is this a technologically useful pursuit?

The Lincoln Navigator, selling at $70,000, features car-like independent rear suspension and crisp steering. If you want car-like suspension, buy a car, for godssake. For $70,000, I want the garage to park it in as well.

Who is making these car design decisions? a woman?

In 1994, there were 43,000 deaths by motor vehicle accidents in the United States, or approximately 15 per 100,000 people per year. This is an effective form of population control.

How many families have had the horror of their sons or daughters being killed in cars driven by irresponsible teen-agers? How many people suffer or suffer with other members of the family who are head injury victims of car accidents? The pain and the loss is hard to explain when development money could be spent on safe vehicles and safe driving laws rather than on male-appealing speed and power and fancy design features. And further, let's just move closer to where we work and quit all this "commuting".

Technology has put people out of work when work is truly necessary to the mental health of a person. The need to contribute meaningfully to the community and be recognized as a useful component of the community has been sacrificed for the technology, which has become a god in itself.

What we are finding, however, is that upgrading that technology to keep up to the techno-industries' developments, to keep functioning when the technology changes is not cost effective. We have computers changing at a rapid pace and the old software is not compatible with the new hardware, and the old hardware can't run the new software. Engineering and architecture firms have invested huge sums of money to get into the computer assisted design (CAD) systems only to find they are soon incompatible with other firms they do business with. To buy these ever-changing and upgrading technologies in order to meet the male solution to the problems, the revolving credit loans guarantee the companies will never actually compute in the black. They could have been paying draftspersons the whole time—probably for less money.

There is currently an observation that the male world is in an identity crisis—which may explain all this extreme sports, and UFC sports mania. On the show *Alpha Male* on Discovery TV channel, they claim that since the birth control pill became available in the 60s, men have lost their bearings because they no longer control female fertility. Interesting. Certainly, the middle-eastern male and some intolerant religions have resisted giving females the right to control their fertility, which seems to be very important to them. With women claiming their reproductive rights, the program claimed, the end all and be all of the male hard-core purpose to inseminate the females and perpetuate the species has become frustrated and men no longer know how to behave. They suggested that male depression and personal crises would seem to bear this out.

There may be something in this, but I don't see that the insemination of females has been so frustrated. We could, however, lay some of the confused male identity to the rise of technology as much as to the birth control pill since many men are delighted not to be burdened with more children than they can afford to support. With technology, however, we have taken the active male and put him in a computer cube farm where he sits all day long like a pumpkin waiting to be carved, his body suffering from lack of activity—thereby frustrating and depressing him. I remember watching a blacksmith when I was waiting for the schoolbus at the age of ten. He was active, working with pride in the blacksmith shop, and I loved to watch.

You can't love to watch someone at a computer or a desk or monitoring machines. We have sensitive men, but now they are frustrated with inactivity, without any tangible products of their talents and abilities and without tangible results for their labors. There is a big rise in home woodworking shops—Lee Valley is doing great, selling upscale to these wannabe carpenters. Many of them are remarkably good at their crafts and can come home from their cube farms and thrive in their workshops. Unfortunately, many can't afford these therapies.

We have, unwittingly, become slaves to technology, and what is happening to those without the necessary computer skills? They are gardeners and garden nursery workers, home care domestics, public maintenance or food industry workers; low paid laborers for the most part, because we have made other mid-range work obsolete.

Men have determined that everything is done better and cheaper, cheaper, cheaper with machines than by human workers who may not meet the robot mentality needed for modern production. Men also like their technical toys and the more ingenious the tools and the electronics or mechanical mechanisms the better. And they ARE ingenious and these innovations are almost indispensable now. In fact, our dependence on our technological helpers was startlingly apparent when there was a terrible cold snap in the north east part of North America—in New York state, and Ontario and Quebec a few years ago; many people went cold and hungry, and some died when their power was cut off and transportation was impossible. In 50-60 years, we have lost our ability to survive the elements without our technology.

These techno-developments have to be carefully assessed since they are not foolproof nor endlessly supportable. And there should be limitations on the excessive developments that squander money for no gain, such as cars that talk, and the many conveniences that keep us from actually moving our bodies.

The male members of the species are not hardwired for these sedentary jobs, for sitting 8-10 hours a day in front of computers or for sitting long hours in classes and lectures. Yet male success is more promising for those who are able to meet these unnatural demands.

Well this is a male world and men are doing these things to themselves. The technology age has been built upon the industrial revolution work-style that enslaves people in work regimens that are killing all of us.

People don't like their lives; they want to stop the world and get off. We aren't happy—we are driven and we don't know why we are unhappy. We buy things but they don't make us happy. We get depressed because we are doing all the things that should make us successful and being successful we should be happy, but we aren't.

What do we all wish for these days?

To win a million dollars.

The TV shows that are so popular are the "win-the-million-dollar" shows—no matter what the ordeal a person has to go through to win the money, we all want to do whatever it takes to get a break from our lives. With a million dollars we can take a break from the rat race that is run by the King Rats; we can stop running on the never-ending treadmill and can look around, breathe, sleep, and meet our own deadlines.

So if our greatest fantasy is to get the million dollars so that we can relax for a few years—what does this say?

It says that the modern male-driven lifestyles are killing us—we hate being enslaved to the hour-shackled axis of commerce that simply gobbles up our energies until we are old, with failing health before we can get off the damned people-eating machines.

Aboriginal people in the outback don't do this. Mothers at home don't do this except to ensure the rest of the family meets the timelines.

Mothers and wives who don't work outside the home work hard, sometimes 12 hours a day 7 days a week, but they can choose to take 3 hours off to visit a friend if they choose to. Is this why women, on average, live longer than men? Work equals stress when there is the imposition of time limitations and quota demands. Time frames, deadlines, quotas, all set by other people on your day, week, month, and year equals stress—bad stress that kills.

Some companies have found that workers are more productive and more efficient and, good lord,—happier—when they can go to work at any time they like. Those who work well in the morning can go to work at 5 or 6am, those who like to stay up at night can do so and go to work at noon. How enlightened. Think of the productivity of people working when they are ready to work.

But no, as a result of serving the GDP economy we have to have a workforce unable to thrive under natural conditions, yet programmed to get out there and be successful.

The second most common prescription prescribed at our university is Prozac. We have to drug our young people so that they can function in this goal-oriented success-demanding society. We have education that forces 18-22 year old males and females to sit on chairs in deadly lecture classes while their hormones are raging and their muscles are atrophying. We are breaking them down psychologically, these wonderful young people, because our society will only reward the winners in this technological freak show.

Men get a sense of value in active engagement with a world that needs their skills, yet we have evolved into a world that doesn't need their vision and ingenuity or their survival skills, their hunt and kill strategies that they inherently need to develop, so the chance of war, the car chase, the promise of the ultimate challenge—extreme sports—is mighty attractive, while at the same time absolutely abhorrent. So again we have a contradictory message and demands on men—and women. As mentioned, we are all going through a huge world-wide identity crisis.

As though the world wasn't already twisted into a pretzel, now we have physicists believing time travel is possible—and are discussing how to build a time machine. And the US Government wants to send more guys to the moon—good grief, we have been there and there wasn't a pub in sight. Is the space industry pitted against the war industries for their fair share of free money? I think the war machine is winning because the moon project is now on hold.

Always, we have to push the envelope—any envelope—and once past these envelopes, we still don't have improved security of life for anyone, we don't have a better civilization, and the irresponsible money grabbers with connections to the comptrollers of our money just move on to the next lucrative envelope.

You don't have to be a Luddite (and I am not a Luddite—I love my computer) to realize there are still many jobs that are done better by human beings, and one of them is answering government and business phones—ironically, especially the telecom industry phones.

(9) MEN & THE MEDIA & ENTERTAINMENT

Twenty years ago in the US, there were 50 owners of all the radio stations (not many, really, since there were 9,254 radio stations in the US in 1989.) In April 2002, there were 5 major owners of radio stations in the US. The big guppy stations have gobbled up all the little guppy stations and a local DJ may in fact be the same *local* DJ in 10 different states.

The megamonopolies now own radio, TV, newspapers, music and cable companies, movie production houses, and publishers, and those few owners can hold advertisers to ransom, charge fees without competition, and take an undesirable control of the program content. These monopolies also monopolize peripheral industries, billboards, concert promotion, and Broadway shows, so that they can demand musical artists sign with them for concerts or they don't get air play on their network of radio stations, virtually guaranteeing the failure of the sales of their records.

This result is an artistic dumbing down to where only "safe" music is distributed—the creativity is determined by financial committees, and successful artists are not able to change their style or the record companies won't carry the CDs. Some mediocre manufactured artists, some of whom are incapable of performing live, are processed in the star machine and spit out on to the top ten charts. The recording industry, however, with the advent of iTunes is now in decline.

To see how incredibly low this trend is taking the culture, we need only look at the TV programming that is saturated with male fantasy. Hour after hour, there are TV cop shows of sleaze and violence, male adventure shows of sleaze, easy sex and violence—and there are never-ending movies of explosions, car chases, sleazy sex, drugs and guns.

Males of all ages are seen having sex with beautiful skinny women—many of these women have bony boy-like bodies which is a particularly disturbing trend, since women try to meet these "desirable" body shapes and become bulimic and anorexic, thereby actually killing themselves for these impossible male fantasies. One university women's soccer team has been depleted of talent because of the low grades of two players, and health reasons for two others— they were bulimic—soccer players were bulimic.

The violence on all these shows is ever more innovative and disgusting. The thrills of the gangster movie has dominated the American culture for more than a generation. The concept of peace and humanitarian coexistence is ludicrous in the face of all these killing images.

The creativity of artists used to reflect society; now these artistic creations are forming society. Consequently, we have a generation that accepts gangsters as the norm in our society, believing the gangsters are the acceptable power leaders of the world. The public believes they are powerless to make changes because the gangsters are calling the shots, and self preservation encourages them to be subservient. The movies as the new religion are delivering a compliant generation of victims.

There are excellent mystery shows and legal shows, but they are few. The trash dominates. Movies like *Swordfish* and *the Departed* are typical examples of gratuitous violence. In *the Departed*, (a good movie, actually, until you think about it) whenever they came to a problem in the script, they killed off another person until by the end they had wasted just about every character with gunfire-in-your-face brutal murder. And the movie was nominated for an Oscar. They glorify the mob and the killing, and they condition the young people to crime and sordid behavior.

Someone somewhere has decided this is what people want. Every show has to have the formula, the male fantasy of the kinky explicit sex in some new kink, the virile muscled alpha male who can leap tall buildings saving Gotham from the evil ones with Barbie skinny women adoring him no matter how devoid he is of personality or physical attraction. (They also have sex without consequences—don't we wish.) And there is the trite overused script, the explosions, always the wild car chase, a few slick and funny lines of dialogue, all created with exceptional production and camera work that convinces the gullible that the film is a worthwhile entertainment. It isn't: it is all flash and trash.

There was a study done on violence in the media and how it increases a person's heart rate. *Newsday* reported a study done by Dr. Murray Mittleman and his colleagues at Harvard Medical School. They discovered that a person's blood pressure goes up when people are exposed to Rambo-style movies. The dose of violence triggers a higher blood pressure surge when an on-screen argument turns into a physical fight. Interestingly, the cardiovascular changes occurred mostly when people watched violence carried out by someone of the same sex, that is, men's pressure went up when men were fighting, and women's pressure went up when women were attacked. The researchers were concerned that these continual artificial blood pressure surges are increasing the risk for cardiovascular disease.

I challenge anybody to sit in front of the TV set and surf across the US channels and NOT find an explicit sex scene and channel after channel with people pointing guns at people. Try to find two comedies that could rival *I Love Lucy* or *the Honeymooners*, the all-time great sitcoms that didn't use violence, cheap sex or skinny boy-like women. We still have this kind of talent—we have writers who can write great scripts for today, but most of the really talented stuff doesn't get past the formula masters who have decreed that only smutty sex and violence sells.

We looked forward for a couple of years to the return of Jason Alexander from *Seinfeld*. Then we got the show *Bob Paterson*, and it was terrible. The premise of the show was so promising, but the script was so shabby, so incongruously sex oriented. How much can you take of a short fat bald man as a sex object? And why would they want to take a man of Alexander's comedic and acting stature and do this to him? This huge talent was metaphorically defanged and shackled and literally forced to dance in his underwear. We wanted his show, but the scripts were impossibly contrived and ridiculous. The same thing happened with Julia Louis-Dreyfuss and Jeffrey Tambor (from Gary Shandling's show) when they tried new vehicles for their talents. All three were criminally trashy shows.

Even in a recent movie set in the boonies of Newfoundland, William Hurt's character snorts cocaine for no other reason than because it was available. There was no artistic need for him to snort cocaine. But the movies condition us to believe that drugs are funny, drugs are smart, cheating people is clever, revenge is honorable, and violence is fun. If you don't laugh, you ain't cool, man.

In the comedy *Analyze This*, starring Billy Crystal and Robert deNiro, which is supposed to appeal to the family, the mobster goes to an intimidated shrink. The message seems to be that mobsters are funny hip guys who make things happen—the movie blatantly glorifies crime and coercion and vice. Also, the Bruce Willis comedy, *The Whole Nine Yards* "A former mob hit man [who else?] becomes a meek dentist's neighbor". It is another movie desensitizing people to the crimes of the bullies. A female character in the movie actually worships the hit man and his reputation, and in her anorexic glory wants desperately to be a hit person just like Willis's character.

Maybe the food channel is our last resort for trash-free entertainment—unless we consider Gordon Ramsey's brand of brutal cuisine.

It isn't just the movies and TV but even the computer games are trading on sleaze. Tomb Raider features a cartoon female who looks more distorted than Barbie with impossible physical dimensions and she tries to find and kill the enemy—zap, kill, knock out and defeat—a booby show as a video game.

Even worse is the Play Station game, *Grand Theft Auto 3* where you, the player, mug, slug, cheat, rob and kill taxi drivers, ethnic people, women, and police officers—you are the thug and the more you club a person, the more blood spurts out.

The commercialization of the media is beyond tolerable limits. Visitors from Europe are incredulous at the *numbers* and *repetition* of the brainwashing cruddy commercials pumped out of American TV sets. Like the frog gradually warmed up in the hot water until he boils, we have been notched up gradually, accepting, accepting. Who do we think is going to put the brakes on this trash-spewing industry?

This is what happens when the men with the most money call all the shots, when they control all the artistic choices. The movie *Get Shorty,* starring John Travolta, was a big eye-opener into the movie-TV production process in which the crime-bosses fund and control the productions. And what are the interests of the underworld? Drugs, sex, violence, brutality, greed, control, cops, crime, and prostitution. So what are 90% of the movies about?—drugs, sex, cops, crime, violence, brutality, greed, control, and prostitution; all are sanitizing crime, vice and the criminal. They have us believing that the normal condition for society is selfish greed and a gun culture. Thank you, Hollywood.

Obviously cigarette money is still backing the movies. I haven't smoked in over 25 years, but I found myself walking out of the movie *Bandits* where Billy Bob Thornton smoked in every scene, thinking hmmmm, smoking looks pretty cool. Johhny Depp smoked and drank his way through the sleeze of Rio in the 2011 movie, *the Rum Diary.* Dr. James Sargent and Dr. Madeline A. Dalton of Dartmouth Medical School, checked the top 25 movies of each year from 1988 to 1997 and found that one-third of the main characters were shown smoking, or lighting up when confiding in others. And these cigarette ad movies were rated PG.

Without drugs, vice or cigarette money backing the movies, few movies get made. Ed Harris spent nine (9) years putting together the money and means to make the movie *Pollock*, a movie that was an incredible insight into the complexities and demons that tormented the artist Jackson Pollack, but the movie was obviously not a favorite for the big financiers. Nine years it took. It probably takes six months to get the financing for most action-packed cigarette, drugs or vice-glorifying movies. Since 9/11, the US military has been backing a lot of the movies, providing free aircraft carriers, jets, bases, etc. to produce recruiting films as entertainment.

"It is just a movie," some of my students protested in support of these violent shows.

Well, no. It isn't. It is constant brainwashing images of irresponsible male behavior that undermines decency in the human race. It is visual affirmations of men gratifying their completely undisciplined appetites, with women as colorful sexy props serving the male agenda.

Real can be entertaining; insightful myths can be entertaining. Real can be funny; male sexual violent fantasy about the basest human behaviour is not entertaining. It is voyeuristic, cheap, tawdry, provocative, and dumbs down the whole culture, and you don't feel clean after watching these shows. One of the first demands of the US trade missions to other countries is to sell these movies. How can these foreign countries not resent this?

David Denby reviewed two movies in the New Yorker, April 2, 2007. His closing statement, "Made in a time of frustration, when Americans are fighting a war that they can neither win nor abandon, '300' and 'Shooter' feel like the products of a culture slowly and painfully going mad."

My only observation here is that it not going so slowly.

Men and women both have to pool their ingenuity to get this death grip of murder, crime, and vice out of the culture. We have to give the people more to strive for and more confidence in their own tastes.

The killing culture has gotta stop.

(10) MEN & THE ENVIRONMENT

When money is the only measure of man's success, status, self-esteem, and power, then the welfare of the people and the welfare of the environment are secondary, if that. All must serve men's short-term needs.

Somehow, modern industry and political leaders have segregated their lives from life. There seems to be no connection between what is done to the planet and the effect on the people who live on the planet or between what people eat, drink and breathe and what diseases they get. Their minds are compartmentalized into two sections:

Section 1: what can I do or use to make myself rich?
Section 2: who has these things and how can I get them?

The fact that leukemia has markedly increased in the last 25-30 years, that there is increasing asthma, allergies, autism, and learning disorders in our children is not part of their consciousness.

Industry takes no responsibility for the chemicals they use in pesticides, fertilizers, carpets, insulation, food packaging, paints, preservatives, and food processing. We now have new rules on the contents of paint, however.

Many of the pesticides on the market are deliberately designed to kill nerve connections, which alter behavior and diminish intelligence, yet somehow the chemical industry insists that the toxins won't affect humans. And governments turn a blind eye when industry frowns, so industry goes unchecked except for occasional showcase examples.

This is how environmental issues are compromised on the large scale. On May 2, 2002, the Government of British Columbia promised to "streamline the forestry code". The forests' minister, Mike de Jong, claimed, "It's time to cut the regulatory burden and make way for a competitive market-based industry." (Times-Colonist, Victoria)

The paper reported,

> "The current Forest Practices Code has rules and plans which are enforced by the province, but the government envisages a new code which would allow companies to decide how to reach certain standards."

This streamlining became necessary because the US imposed punishing illegal duties on Canada's softwood exports which has put thousands out of work and decimated BC's largest export industry, and in this atmosphere of urgency, this streamlining measure to get rid of much paperwork looked very appealing.

Now this is fine, getting rid of the increased overburden of government inefficiency, but giving the logging companies the right to set their own rules and govern themselves looks like another move to simply dispense with regulations.

If they will (or even if they *might*) lose money because of some environmental concern, can we seriously expect any company to choose to lose money? Enforcement of the rules would only come after the damage has been done.

We have seen many times how the companies take advantage of every covert opportunity to take the easiest and cheapest means of deforesting the Province. In the summer of 1993, we had 932 citizens arrested for standing on a logging road committing "civil disobedience". Many of these brave people went to jail trying to protect 262,000 hectares of old growth forests in the Clayoquot Sound, one of the largest tracts of temperate rainforest remaining on Earth. The princes of the government, the police, and the huge forest industries were united in their condemnation of these people who were defending the rain forest, and pressed for prosecution, which the courts delivered—a mass trial never seen before in Canada that included two grandmothers. In fact, this was the largest mass trial in the western world.

Robert F. Kennedy, Jr. commented that these individuals "practiced civil disobedience to make governments more just and democratic." Would that it were true.

Lawyer, Ron McIsaac, who voluntarily defended many of the protesters, stated that the proposed clear-cutting of the forest is a ". . . story of waste. One thousand-year-old trees are replaced by tiny potted plants."

Here are two other quotes on the destruction of the environment by our society:

> "Rainforests are, in effect, 'the lungs of the planet,' helping to regulate the exchange of oxygen and carbon dioxide, just as our own lungs do. In the Amazon region alone, 75 billion tons of carbon are filtered out of the air by trees . . . Ecologists are convinced we are the last generation that has a chance to save [rainforests]."
> Anita Gordon and David Suzuki, 1990.

"We must bring environmentally damaging activities under control to restore and protect the integrity of the Earth's systems we depend on. No nation can escape from injury when global biological systems are damaged."

Union of Concerned Scientists, (a group of senior members of the world's scientific community), 1992.

The dangers of our life style and our market-driven world order is well known to most high-school, college and university students, yet our governments continue to ride shotgun for the business interests who want to convert everything on the planet into a revenue source.

Shortly before Sept 11'ths attacks (2001), VP of the USA, Dick Cheney, announced that the US was not going to look into conservation measures, that the Bush government was going to find the energy resources the American people have come to expect, and they would develop those resources. Then we had 9-11 (was there a connection?); then there were developers moving into the state of Wyoming to extract coal bed methane in Powder River Valley from under many of the farms. Most of those farmers didn't own the mineral rights under their farms, so the coal bed operators simply moved onto their lands with the $3B development money from the US government and set up their pumps. This operation has destroyed much of the surrounding lands with the associated pollution. The Bush Government approved 80,000 such wells over a 10 year period.

Concerned scientists can ring the alarm bells 'til the cows come home (if there are any left out on the range) and none of the governments will respond. Even California, one of the greatest consumers of power and water and energy, yet one of the foremost states in its environmental laws, is at the mercy of the mega-corporations who have wily lawyers challenging any laws that get in their way.

Environmentalists have projected that by 2050, the planet will no longer sustain the people living on it.

We have bovine growth hormones in the cow's milk. And we have vitamins and calcium added to the milk, and then the milk is advertised as a rich source of calcium for those at risk of osteoporosis. They don't tell you that the calcium they add to the milk may not be as assimilable to the human system as the natural milk calcium or that milk could actually contribute to the development of osteoporosis. They don't point out that we are the only species in the world that drinks milk after babyhood.

They don't tell you that sedatives can deplete the body's calcium, and that all these older women taking sleeping pills could be increasing their risk of getting osteoporosis with these pills.

Recently, the milk industry was advocating the weight-reduction benefits of milk. When milk is comprised of hormones that promote fat, this has to be a contender for the Biggest Lie competition. "Don't believe the hype," Dr. Amy Joy Lanou told Reuters Health. "The ads that promote milk as helping to achieve a healthy weight are misleading; the science does not support these claims."

Most of our fruit and vegetables have been bioengineered. This hybridizing form of altering our produce is not necessarily all bad. Some of it, however, can have long term consequences to the crops and to the biodiversity of species. Also, any genetic alteration can be patented and then that species becomes a corporate asset to be sold at whatever prices. The monopolies sell wheat growers bioengineered suicide seed that will not grow fertile seeds for sowing the next season, thereby forcing the farmers to buy their seeds every year at high prices from the seed merchants. Farmers who don't cooperate have been taken to court for growing their own crops.

All of our foods are now commodities and have come under the control of the predatory food industry marketeers, primarily because people always have to eat, and so, by controlling the supply for a never-ending demand, they are guaranteed never-ending profits.

This is not good for farmers and countries who would like to feed themselves.

The newspapers are certainly one of the most wasteful of all; they publish newspapers that need trucks to deliver them to the homes. How many people read all of these papers before throwing them out? I take the flyer-filled local free paper from the front door, glancing at it as I carry it to the backdoor where I put it into the recycling bin.

Cut trees (ecodamage)—process into pulp and paper (ecodamage, pollution)—sell ads (profit)—print newspapers (pollution)—deliver (pollute)—throw out within 24 hours (ecodamage).

The newsprint eats up the trees that are part of the forests which provide a CO_2 sink that converts the air into usable air for other living species. We were supposed to end up with a *paperless society* when the personal computer (pc) was introduced. We would do well to limit every newspaper to 10 pages maximum and then we might find out what is worth reporting and what is just fear-mongering and trouble-making to provide pages for ads.

The transportation sector of our society accounts for 25% of the greenhouse gas emissions. The car industry could improve these levels and have been working on this—apparently. We don't see much happening very fast, yet we do see lots of new models coming on the market regularly. And all the car makers copy each other so that we have 6 companies putting out identical models to each other but few of them putting out a different car.

Thirty years ago, we had a big oil/gas crisis—major shortages in which people were lining up at gas stations in the US at 4am hoping to get gas. People actually shot each other for jumping the line—well they had guns in their cars to do it. So most of the people with their big cars with all that metal to protect themselves bought small efficient compact cars that the car companies just happened to have ready to sell. You could buy an old luxury Cadillac or Lincoln for $600. Then, for no reason that we heard of, there was lots of gas again but the price had gone up. Two groups gained significantly from that gas shortage; the car industry and the oil industry.

Then when everyone was scurrying around in the smaller cars, the government realized that cities were having number 3 alert smog problems and set limits on passenger car gas emissions that needed catalytic converters to reduce the worst of the toxic emissions. Again, the car industry complied and sold thousands of catalytic converters, plus more little market-boosting cars.

Then curiously, when the gas shortage had faded from the buyer's minds, auto companies, needing to keep up their market share, appealed to the male fantasy as marketing gurus always do. Most people had moved off the farm and were living in cities but cities make you nostalgic for the open road, the bigger spaces. They came up with the 4x4 for the males to go off-road. These were a hit, so they started marketing vans and SUVs and light trucks as family vehicles—again, safer, of course, with more metal to protect the little woman and the kids. (The same old sell as in the 50s). And men bought the fantasy portrayed in the commercials that showed the vehicles careening around rural corners, over bumps, through lake-sized puddles, around mountain corners, and more corners and more corners. It didn't matter that most men never drive off-road, and some of those 4x4s were found to be actually unstable—unsafe. But, no matter, the male self-image was gratified. These vehicles are big gas guzzlers, however, yet the companies didn't seem to have any trouble selling them. Why not? Because the emission standards were set for *passenger cars*, not trucks and SUVs and vans that are classified as *trucks*. So, again, the oil companies and the car industry made big gains burning more and more fossil fuels—with impunity.

Government shuts a blind eye to the loopholes that big business crawls through, in this instance, the auto industry. They could have closed the loophole that exempted the big vehicles from the emission regulations, but curiously, they still haven't done that.

Now that the market is almost saturated with the big wheels, you can bet your hulking chunk of metal that one of two things will happen soon. There will be another oil/gas shortage (or, as it turns out, there is a huge bump in the price of gas) and all those people with the big wheels like the Ford Excursion that cost over $3000/year for gas, will dump the heavy metal and buy new efficient hybrids or the new little gas efficient cars,

OR *t*he government will close up the "loophole" in the emissions' regulation governing truck class vehicles (with a mock protest from the auto industry), and all those people owning the big wheels will have to comply by buying the new smaller cars that the car industry will almost certainly be poised to sell.

And, again, the car industry gains just when the market is starting to slow down.
(See http://autosmart.nrcan.gc.ca/ for fuel efficiency information.)

There is a long list of greed and consequences that stretches across the ages from the ivory trade to the Bengal tiger trade to the decimation of the rainforest to the pollution of the waterways to the acid rain destruction of the sugar maples to the desertification of the crop areas in many of the California produce lands and elsewhere, most of which is male-driven.

For example: males of European origin killed all the buffalo in the US in the 1800s so they could create a cow-meat market that they could make money from because they couldn't make money if everyone had free buffalo meat. In the 1860s, reportedly 6 million buffalo were killed, many by recreational shooting parties on the trains. This was a tourist attraction. Buffalo Bill Cody killed 4,280 buffalo himself. Killing the buffalo also starved the indians who could not exist freely on the land ever again. Then the white settlers ran stock—farmed beef—which put everyone's food source behind fences and in their bank accounts.

Reverend John Beckewelder lived with the Pennsylvania Indians and wrote about the natives he knew there in 1819:

"They think that [God] made the earth and all that it contains for the common good of mankind . . . Whatever liveth on the land, whatsoever groweth out of the earth, and all that is in the rivers . . . was given jointly to all, and everyone is entitled to his share . . . hospitality . . . is not a virtue but a strict duty.

"They give and are hospitable to all, without exception, and will always share with each other and often with the stranger, even to their last morsel. They would rather lie down themselves on an empty stomach, than have it laid to their charge that they had neglected their duty by not satisfying the wants of the stranger, the sick or the needy . . . for if the meat they had been served with, was taken from the woods, it was common to all before the hunter took it; if corn or vegetables, it had grown out of the common ground, yet not by the power of man, but by that of the Great Spirit. Besides, on the principle that all are descended from one parent, they look upon themselves as but one great family, who therefore ought at all times and on all occasions, to be serviceable and kind to each other . . ."

No wonder the First Nation's people fell afoul of our laws, thinking that everything on the earth was god's and free to humans to take if they needed it. Our laws guarantee individual ownership of everything on the planet with a price on every item that a man lays claim to, violently protected by police forces.

You can't help feeling a huge sorrow for the loss of such a world order as that of the Pennsylvania natives. They had their flaws and do have their flaws, but so much that was good in many of the tribes has been criminally expunged.

(I remember talking to one couple from Northern British Columbia who woke one morning to find a Native Indian sleeping on the couch in their living room. He had been in the small town partying on the weekend and needed a bed to sleep on. Hospitality was taken for granted.)

The hunter-gatherer is still there, in me anyway. Every spring and every fall I get restless. The natives in these parts used to have their summer residences and their winter residences as the cycle of fish and game dictated. Maybe having lived all my life in the same territory, I have absorbed these instincts. I compulsively pick blackberries every year—wonderful free food—and I make jam for the winter or freeze lots of fruit. I seem to be subject to all the urges the human species ever had.

The first year after I graduated, I had to work 12 months in the same place doing the same job. No more changes of job in the spring and fall. I found this to be very difficult—nearly had a breakdown. And then it went on the next year and the next year.

Many of the aboriginal tribes on the planet today only "work" about 3-4 hours a day to provide themselves with sustenance. So our lifestyle is not only killing the animals, destroying species diversity that is essential to continuing adaptation of the living forms, damaging the planet, and threatening our physical health, it is creating so much stress in our lives that we can barely function without little "helpers" like alcohol or drugs of some kind—mostly prescription.

Because we can see the increasing destruction of our planet and quality of our lives, we simply can't leave it in the hands of these ruthless shortsighted money-grabbing marketeers.

It's gotta stop.

(11) HISTORY & ZOOLOGY

It is fine to identify problems, but without reasonable do-able solutions, the criticisms are irresponsible.

So, what do we do?

With almost overwhelming odds against easing the male death-grip on the civilizations on the planet, how can we make a difference? How do we stop the greed and the enmity and the arrogance and the brutality of not just our young men when their hearts are black, but of our old men when their hearts are still power hungry?

Does this male perspective on the social order always have to be the same? And was it always like this?

Other civilizations

There have been societies on earth in which there has been relative stability, in which the human race flourished and wars were at a minimum.

The ancient historical evidence and prehistory evidence indicates that there was probably a 2000 year period of relative peace and prosperity in the middle east between 3500 and 1500 BC when the reverence for birth and life was the guiding principle.

One of those times was the Minoan period, on the Island of Minos off the coast of Greece, from about the 3000-1500 BC. There is substantial evidence in Malta, then in Crete, in Hungary, Anatolia (Turkey) and the Greek mainland of a very long stable peaceful society that did not focus on war, weapons and death. Their civilization was highly developed with paved roads, indoor plumbing, irrigation systems, good housing with tiled and plastered walls both for the priestesses and priests and the workers. They were highly sophisticated artists with excellently wrought gold cups, pottery that has still not been duplicated, small sculptures and delicate frescoes. Women had a place of influence and were able to counterbalance the excesses of male needs and behavior.

Indeed, their religion had primarily female goddesses.

Both men and women participated in the same sports, and inheritance appears to have been through the females. There is evidence that even poor areas of town had social equality with distribution of wealth—the rich and the poor thrived.

The Minoans raised cattle, sheep, pigs, and goats, grew wheat, barley, vetch, and chickpeas, cultivated grapes, figs, olives, and poppies, and domesticated bees.

Egypt also had many years of stability and constructive civilization. During many of those years, women ruled in tandem with the men, sometimes with more, sometimes with less power than the men.

Those ancient societies in which women had status came to a nasty end when the civilization was threatened by external forces and men rushed into battle to save their worlds for the little woman and children by killing the bad guys, (and other women and children), and the societies never regained the equilibrium they had previously enjoyed.

Whenever there was a balance of power between the sexes, the people and the communities flourished. Whenever men are overly predominant, there have been wars and cultures destroyed.

Various tribes of native indians in North America also enjoyed many generations of fairly peaceful existence when the warriors weren't painting their faces black. In 1709, John Lawson, a surveyor, spent time with the Indians in North Carolina. The natives were certainly not non-violent but women were respected and contributed a civilizing effect. Lawson observed that if a marriage broke up and the woman took up with another man, the children went with the mothers, who obviously had rights over their choice of marriage, choice to leave the marriage, and rights to the children. The women chose who to sleep with all at times and the community accommodated those choices, and in that egalitarian society, an indian man never married so near as a first cousin. If the tribe was small (as happened after the white killers arrived) they looked for partners amongst strangers.

> "For if an Indian lies with his Sister, or any very near Relation, his body is burnt, and his ashes thrown into the River, as unworthy to remain on Earth . . ."

Lawson:

> "The woman is not punished for Adultery, but tis the Man that makes the injured Person Satisfaction, which is the Law of Nations, . . . and he that strives to evade such Satisfaction as the Husband demands, lives daily in danger of his Life, yet when discharged, all Animosity is laid aside, and the Cuckold is very

well pleased with his Bargains, whilst the rival is laughed at by the Whole Nation."

Look at the contrast between responsibility by the man for his actions as opposed to that of the Hebrew, Christian, Muslim, Chinese, or Hindu behaviour and judge which society is civilized—the uncivilized modern man throwing stones at defenseless women, or the civilized savage. These modern males blame and punish women for every male transgression, and the children are taken from any woman they choose to discard.

Further, Lawson wrote,

> the males ". . . are never to boast of their Intrigues with the women. If they do, none of the Girls value them ever after, or admit of their company in their beds."

> "Though we may reckon them [the women] the greatest Libertines; yet they retain and possess a Modesty that requires those Passions never to be divulged."

We lament that in the marauding onslaught of the Western scourge, they blindly destroyed all that was good in the culture clash and retained all that gave them bully rights in both white and indian societies.

Thomas Morton, another Indian observer in New England in 1632 wrote,

> "According to human reason, guided onely by the light of nature, these people leades the more happy and freer life, being voyde of care, which torments the mindes of so many Christians . . . [and] . . . A basket cake given to one: that one breakes it equally into so many parts as there be persons in his company, and distributes it."

The circumpolar religions of the aboriginal peoples did not exalt humans above the rest of creation, thus the males were not exalted above the female.

The Ojibway worshipped the earth mother with tobacco pouch offerings to the mother.

The Iroquois (which included 5 tribes including the Algonquin and Seneca in what is now New York State), had a role for the great goddess as well as Thunderer, the male god, each with complementary roles.

The Zuni Indians in the southwest of America were matrilinear and the houses and cornfields were owned by the women, (unlike the Rio Grande Indians who were patrilinear.)

As one medicine man stated;

> "We are a product of mother and father. For every breath we breathe, and for every ray of sunshine, we give thanks to the father, and for every step we take and for every growing thing we revere the mother."

Also, one elder advised that all should learn about *natural interrelatedness*, and no one should interfere with the ceremonies of any other tribe. That gives us pause to think about our modern pushy violent, proselytizing religions.

We have many instances in history in which there have been more caring, happier times for large numbers of people. We lost them because men have usurped the power for selfish greed. Think about that Minoan society 1600 years before Christ that had paved roads and indoor plumbing. When my parents were children, they didn't have indoor plumbing. We lost all that ancient technology and we could lose it again.

Making changes, however, in which one group has to sacrifice for the greater good, is nearly impossible.

As Martin Luther King Jr. wrote in his letter from Birmingham Jail in 1963,

> "Lamentably, it is an historical fact that privileged groups seldom give up their privileges voluntarily. Individuals may see the moral light and voluntarily give up their unjust posture; but, as Reinhold Niebuhr has reminded us, groups tend to be more immoral than individuals."

Other species

Since we don't seem to be the most intelligent species on the planet by the evidence of our inclination to destroy ourselves, maybe we can look at other species to see how they have survived for so long.

The elephant species, definitely a highly civilized species, has evolved a workable culture—if man would stop killing them. The male elephants are turned out of the herd when they become testosterone-driven males. The matriarchal women run the communities and the males are welcome only when the species needs to procreate. The male elephant is seen as a threat and though he has his hierarchy among the males, their behavior is not allowed to disrupt the ongoing pursuits and needs of the females and offspring. There appears to be an understanding that the needs of the male elephant are not particularly compatible with the survival of the species.

When I asked one man, what do men want? He replied, "to be left alone."

Maybe we should talk to the elephants.

The killer whales (Orcas) have a societal structure similar to ancient human society back when the resident agricultural people seemed to have a fairly stable society and the transient nomads lived on the periphery of the resident civilizations, until the Attila the Hun type of men started murdering and pillaging.

Well the killer whales have similar resident communities here in the Pacific Northwest, with large pods of 30 to 40 whales, while transient nomad pods that have only 6-8 whales continually circle around Vancouver Island. These two groups do not associate with each other. The residents have a good community life and seem to have learned survival by not tolerating the aberrant behavior of the antisocial members of the species. The transient whales are simply not part of the larger killer whale society—outcasts.

Perhaps there is a model there for a peaceful society. Those who won't support a healthy society are cast out.

In our society of marauding international corporations and warlords, all the resident males are as helpless as the women and children in the face of the dominance of these ruthless men who respect nothing and no one. When they own the armies and the weapons, the peace-loving are no match.

When a nomad, with selfish interests that he is convinced are his by right, gets the taste of blood (or the smell of easy money) like any pitbull, there is no return to the herbivore appetites. Most often, an animal—the pitbull, the bear, the cougar—that has developed a lust for human blood is destroyed. The vampire and the werewolf legends are all about the human who gets a lust for blood; that once a man gets a taste for blood, for killing, for brutality, he is a werewolf to be hunted and confined or killed.

Well that is what we have loose in the world at the moment; a whole pack of werewolves appearing to be the good males and the benevolent leaders, while they run amok, destroying lives, communities, nations, and the whole damn planet. Unfortunately, these humans with blood lust in today's society are decorated with medals and rewards.

Herman Golleb, the writer and editor, had to learn all the great villain speeches in Shakespeare as a youth. His dad said he was to memorize those speeches because . . .

> "When you grow up, you are going to run into a lot of greedy, vicious, selfish, envious hombres, and they are going to be very very smart and very sneaky, and they are going to make you think they are your friends, but whenever they get a chance they are going to stab you in the back and take everything you got."

Given that as a fairly realistic assessment of the current leading members of our society, can we hope for 10 seconds that these men (and some women) will change without being forced to do so?

How did the ancients control the brutes?—a vial of poison here or there and a well-placed asp was not unheard of.

How can we outlaw the weapons? If there are no weapons, the flat-brained leaders and politicians will have to resort to some other means to settle disputes, finding some new bloodless ideas.

When asked what caused the first world war, Franz Kafka said, "a huge lack of imagination."

Can we imagine a world without arms, without killing? Can we imagine other means of conflict resolution?

Gandhi advocated truth force; transform conflict, not suppress it or explode it into violence. Such truth force requires a lot of patience, which is the most difficult virtue—because patience takes a long time, and do we have a long time? But patience is said to be the key to the universe, so instead of castrating the misguided male leaders in the world, we may have to get in their faces as often as possible, sit on their doorsteps 24 hours a day, put mirrors up in front of them so that they can see their murderous greed for what it is, strew the banana peels, use our imagination, convince them that power over others and buying more and more male baubles does not make them noble, and noble is highly desirable.

(12) THE 50/50 SOLUTION

So what we have to do is make humanitarian behavior very desirable. We have to confer high esteem on those who improve the living conditions of all people. We do have the numbers, and with the computer technology, we can rally many people in a short time, and with some organization, maybe we can take back the planet from the greedy and brutal.

Suggestions & Options

I do think the first thing we have to do is get the attention of the men in world.

I remember a story my father told when I was a child about a time he went to collect a bill from one of his customers, a farmer. To get to the man's tractor, my dad and the farmer had to go through a field where a huge bull was pastured. Dad was reluctant. "Don't worry," said the farmer, and he picked up a 2x4 board and let the bull have a crack on the forehead with the board, and they proceeded to walk across the pasture with no trouble from the bull.

So, we have to get their attention first, and maybe even render the bullies slightly insensible if we want to move ahead to a greener pasture.

We need women involved in the running of the communities and the countries, and the world, but we don't want women running everything—for many reasons.

o   women can get into some pretty petty spaces that can also be very destructive, and they often lack the ability to see the larger picture that many men seem to have.
o   often, when women get into power roles, they take on the male persona and become Margaret Thatchers, acting more like men than men because they have given up their own sensibilities for those they don't understand. Or perhaps it is the structure that corrupts, a structure created by males. Once in the structure, your behavior is compromised. Men with boobs, my daughter calls these male-type women.
o   most women don't really want power roles. I know three women, a lawyer, an administrator, and a social worker who were given the opportunities to move into senior executive positions, and all three turned them down. They did not want to be committed to the demands of the job, whereas many men will happily submerge themselves in the 12 hour a day job. If these positions didn't make such inhuman demands on the executive, the women could flourish in these positions.
o   if we had women running the world, we would have reciprocating male backlashes like the liberal-conservative backlashes.

So we don't want the mythical amazon woman in total control; we want men contributing, but we have to ensure that they contribute in a *life supporting* fashion. We have to address the needs of all members of the species.

Three actions (wild or otherwise) come to mind.

1) **We can appeal to the competitive nature of men.**

We can appeal to the male pursuit of honor and achievement by bestowing the greatest honors in the world on those who provide care, housing, and food for the greatest number of people without environmental damage.

We would need a value scale, a Real Standard of Living (RSL) measure that I mentioned, that measures the per capita of homeless people, per capita of children and women living below the poverty line, per capita of prisoners, per capita of seniors without decent care, food and housing, per capita of young people without livable wage jobs. The challenge would be to improve the RSL in communities and nations.

The community winners will move on to an international RSL Olympics.

The country whose teams succeed in raising their starting RSL will win world tours and honors in every country—state dinners, for heaven's sake.

We could televise the annual tours of nations and the UN would monitor the honesty and investigate the claims made.

We would celebrate the Real Standard of Living days every year with a worldwide 3 days of festivities. The challenges would be similar to the logging sports in Oregon, Washington and British Columbia, perhaps, with teams showing

o how quickly and efficiently they can build a house for four people.

- o how efficiently they can provide a good holiday for a family of four.
- o how they can reduce the energy needs of a community of 3000.
- o how they can save a tree.
- o how they can feed the homeless.
- o how they can encourage population controls

We can make it *honorable* to care for the people in a nation and care for the environment, with great prestige and status for the most successful.

We have to challenge the men to take their responsibilities as leaders more seriously than any other concern, more seriously than their sports, more seriously than their toys, more seriously than their wars. They will meet the challenge if there is enough glory in being on the team tackling the vices and criminal neglect on the planet.

Some years back, and maybe still today, the RCMP in Canada were like the caretakers of the communities. They tried to make sure everything was running smoothly and fairly, and they were truly loved and respected.

On a trip across British Columbia only a few years ago, I had been driving down the highway and decided to stop at a wooded campground for a break. I walked over to take a look at the creek and slipped on the muddy bank, but I saved myself from landing on my back. Shortly after, a man came along and slipped at the same spot. I called over and we struck up a conversation. He was asking me a few things, and then I was telling him how I had worked out the perfect drive—I would set my cruise control at 3-5 km/hr over the speed limit and the slow drivers never caught up to me and the speeders would fly right past. I had the beautiful drive all to myself. As I was getting to the end of this little explanation it dawned on me very clearly that he was an off duty RCMP officer. And I had just told him that I speed. Anyway, he cautioned me about stopping in such places as the campground by myself. He managed to refrain from telling me not to talk to strangers.

But he reminded me of the security that was so wonderful in those small towns policed by such men as this RCMP officer; you felt safe with such marvelous men in charge. (Not all of them, of course; one I met in Banff was seriously disturbed, but all the others I ever met were superb people.)

How could you not feel nostalgic for such times when such men knew so much more than policing, and were willing to take on huge responsibilities and make such personal sacrifices?

2) We can resort to a general strike.

Mother's Day could become a day of global action. No longer will it be a once a year day of trinkets and smiles and one-day cooperation with Mom. It will be a day to honor all mothers, grandmothers, daughters, and granddaughters who will be the mothers of the future, to honor their right to bring up families in a decent safe environment.

It will also be a day to mourn the loss of our sons, husbands, fathers and our sisters to the insane warmongering of men.

And pro-actively, women will use this special day to take civil action, making loud noises in every city, community and home.

And if Mother's Day, 2012, has no effect on men, then the next Mother's Day in 2013 will be the first day of a global women's strike of inaction and harassment that will continue non stop to the next Mother's Day if necessary.

Women all over the world could refuse to do anything for men, no typing, no cooking, no secretarial work, no airline reserving, no clothes washing, no cleaning, **no sex**, no conversation, no pounding taro, no faxing, no research, nothing for men.

A strike would be a huge wake-up call.

The world will grind to a stop because nothing really happens in this world without the work of women. Though many men are becoming more self-sufficient, most of them are hopelessly unaware of what women do that enables them to function in their so-important positions. It is a fact that many men have no idea what actually happens in their own offices.

In ancient Greece in the 5th Century BC, Aristophanes wrote a play, *Lysistrata,* about the women in the warring city of Athens who decided to unite in refusing their husbands all sexual favors until all war weapons were laid aside. In the play, the men retaliate, but the women win out. Obviously, the women didn't win off the stage, but Aristophane's play gave expression to his dream of salvation for his war-ravaged city after 20 years of the Peloponnesian Wars, wars that virtually ended the Greek civilization.

He is not forgotten, and we have to take up the cause and make it happen this time before we have the wars that do end the world's civilization.

So our strike could include withholding sexual pleasures. We will create a prostitute survival fund to help those in the sex trade survive the strike.

The sex deprived male is an interesting phenomenon. Ask the women of Liberia.

Women in all their groups, church groups, book clubs, school groups, bowling teams, business clubs, will have to take on the role of action groups; they will have to dialog seriously on the actions they can take to do this.

Many, many major developments started with people talking together in the kitchen.

We have the numbers; we only need the will to do this. We need the mutual support to dare to take the actions necessary, *to trust ourselves and other women* to make the demands.

3) We have to outlaw the arms trade and all weapon production and ownership.

Charles Krauthammer wrote an article,
"Peacekeeping is for Chumps" in which he stated that

> "Peace can only be achieved by hegemony or balance of power. It is achieved not by reason, not by dialogues, not by peacekeeping, not by the UN, not by multilateralism."

Not so, Charles, peace cannot be achieved as long as men run the world, and as long as there are huge profits to be gained from the sale of armaments.

The death merchants do control the world, and most likely **start** and **prolong** most of the wars in the world.

1)
We have to demand that the UN declare weapons a global crime against humanity, the criminal being anyone who owns, trades, manufactures or uses weapons for anything but hunting.

We could offer huge rewards to the bounty hunters who bring in the criminals.

The punishments must fit the crime. The manufacturers of landmines will have to go in and clear Europe, Cambodia, Vietnam, Afghanistan, and most of Africa of their mines. The workers in weapons production will have to care for the crippled and maimed for the rest of their lives.

2)
We need to gather the momentum that is necessary to make this leap of change, a critical mass of opinion to effect a paradigm shift.

We know that systems break down in times of extreme imbalance and they are replaced by other systems. Chaos is necessarily unpredictable and occurs after periods of steady state conditions.

For example, you may have a household that progresses in an orderly fashion, and then a small incident that no one saw coming may happen that tears the whole household apart. The small incident may simply be a new item that comes on the market, or there is a change in supplies because one country offends another. Then the dad may lose his job, then the kids can't continue their education, the wife has to take a job where she falls in love with a coworker, the marriage splits up, there is great acrimony between sons and daughters and parents and they all thrash around and find other arrangements.

Then all things may settle down for a period of relative calm and healing—until the next chaotic situation.

The weather is a wonderful example of a chaotic system. The weather may be quite predictable, varying within a normal range, and then some small factor disrupts the pattern and a devastating hurricane occurs wreaking unpredictable damage.

We see how people take advantage of such times of social disruption and chaos. How many governments have fallen to dictators after a coup when the controlling mechanism that imposes the rule of justice is disconnected? Think about the breakup of the Soviet Union.

Political groups often deliberately create chaos in order to effect a political "coup". Governments in one country will create chaos in another to create a "coup" and gain power.

But times are coming unraveled now as people gradually learn that their governments are almost always working against them, that we need to constantly protest to keep the government from ruining the country, and as more and more people realize this, there will come a time of chaos. Such times have spawned bloody revolutions or bloodless coups or simply changes in government direction.

Whatever the trigger, chaos can bring about an even worse condition as has been seen in many African and South American nations. Or the aftermath could result in great changes of improvement if we are poised to take direct advantage of the chaos.

If we can keep the idea of power as responsibility (and not exclusively for oppression and male domination) growing in the societal consciousness, we may be able to make some changes. One major change is to ease the society out of its current anti-human market-crazed lifestyle, and we can do it by changing all work conditions to worker-friendly conditions thereby breaking the anger-breeding conditions. This would also reduce the production of so much useless junk. I am no communist; I am a pragmatist, ready to take what fair trade will provide while embracing human-friendly developments.

We need to change all our education processes to be learning motivated—nothing else. We help people learn at all stages of their lives, and we help them learn well.

3)

We have lots of really brutal precedents in the Bible and the Koran that we could resurrect and adapt for modern times.

We could have a worldwide Passover in which any man who has been violent, has abused women or children, has actively restricted women's rights, who has wantonly wasted natural resources, who has engaged in any activity that has *promoted war or made war possible* (making, buying, selling or using weapons) will be marked by the Angel of Death.

We could declare a jihad against all men who do not support equal rights for all. That would eliminate a huge portion of the destructive element in society, while empowering those men who silently despise the corrupt society they live in.

But do we want to resort to the male sense of retaliation? We might have to, until we rid the society of the violence-loving brutes.

4)

We could practice some genetic engineering—engineering and science is always appealing. Not Nazi genocide or any kind of ethnic cleansing. No killing.

We would selectively breed the human race from a stock of *good men*, selecting for traits from all races and cultures that actively promote the survival of the human race.

We would clean the scum out of the gene pool with a selective stud farm. Only the chosen studs (George Clooney comes to mind) would be allowed to procreate—the other males can have sex but no offspring.

These ideas are going to appeal to different personalities, but we probably need a more do-able change that will move the world toward a long-lasting solution.

The Fifty/Fifty Solution

Probably the only practical step in a civilized process, in the evolution of democracy, is the 50/50 solution.

The Fifty-Fifty Solution:

**The 50/50 solution is a dual-leadership solution.
Every election would elect one female and one male for every office and constituency.**

We would reduce the number of ridings by 50%. Then we would put forth two slates of candidates in every riding; a male choice and a female choice.

There would be one male and one female at the head of every government, co-Prime Ministers, Co-Presidents, Co-sheiks(if necessary), co-premiers, and so on.

Indeed, no country would have UN membership unless they had two equal his & her rulers in their countries.

There would be free votes on every issue and no party restraints on any member.

1)
Inspector Morse on the TV mystery show said on one show, "femininity is a guarantee of civilization", and this we need.

2)

We have studies published that demonstrate when boards of corporations have 3 or more women on the board, the board members were less aggressive, more responsive to different ideas and were more concerned with the reputation of the company. And perhaps foremost, their actions were more humanitarian.

3)

Also, the women need to get one hand on the purse strings. The power to make changes is always determined by the money. Things change at an amazing rate when something is not good for the money-holders. We tend to think there will be a big lag before a change is effected, but that is only so when there is no will to make changes. When McDonald's was pressured to give up the styrofoam containers (in America), once they made the decision to appease the noisy environmentalists, the cups were gone in two weeks.

Follow the money if you want to know who is destroying this world, and get control of the money if you want to make any changes. Dual government leadership guarantees that women will have access to the money and a real voice in how it is spent.

4)

We desperately need a partnership society, a dual leadership society, because we are male and female, the two halves of humanity.

The emphasis and focus of this manifesto/rant is not the jobs' issue. Women's role is to control and counteract the excessive effects of male testosterone—it is the civilizing of men that women need to do—not castrating them. We want men who are men,—at least, I do—but we also want to channel those male excesses mentioned earlier in the book, to harness the antisocial aspects of the male tribe defender. We need to take the wild males and put limits on their excesses and turn them into supporters of the species.

Most women have always done this, of course, but some women are intimidated by their men, mostly because men are fearsome in their angry tantrums and demands and violence. If you find a good-natured peace-loving man, sit him down and wash his feet with your hair.

On the other hand, some women think they must beat a man down—make him communicate like a counselor, and they think this is making him into a compatible human being. This is not so. Often this is repressing a male, this is denaturing the man, and it backfires with more selfish behavior, more porn, more abusive behavior.

Though most of us would just as soon let the men make the decisions because they do have the energy and the single-mindedness to focus on the problems and solve those problems, we can't give them the sole privilege of running the world.

Good childcare at the work sites should be obligatory where mothers can spend their lunch hours with their children. Women should be able to take their babies into the office when necessary and not lose their jobs. With childcare, women can learn the skills necessary to understand the workings of governance.

And women should be able to cry in frustration and not be mocked for their sensitivity. The HBO TV show, *The Closer*, with Kyra Sedgwick as Chief Inspector of the LAPD Major Crimes division, shows so well how a woman who can cry over her cat and fill her office desk with sweet treats can also be a very effective crime solving leader of men.

The women must make sure that most of the government monies are designated for food, shelter, health and education not war and trade of useless materialistic junk, and not for the greed of individuals.

We need to combine the nurturing aspect of the female with the problem-solving skills of the male to develop a viable society. And we need to adopt the Ojibway criteria for decisions and changes—any practice or any change must not compromise the planet for the next 7 generations. If it will, the change does not happen. We have to stop stealing from our descendants. What kind of a parent doesn't want their children to have a good life? Well, we have to stop the killing, the violence, and the waste so that our children and their children and their children can survive. Nothing men have done so far indicates they have even thought of such a responsibility. Too many men want to play cops and robbers and bang-bang all their lives.

So we have to make these changes, and we can, and let's hope we can do this before the bullies blow up the world.

We gotta stop the madness.
We gotta stop the killing.

SOURCES

page

Chapter 1

1   *Prince Harry goes to war* . . . Jill Lawless. Associated Press. Feb 29, 2008. Canwest News Service. 2/29/08 Vancouver sun. A11

3   *Uncle John's Bathroom Reader.* #12.

3   Global Crossing, Enron, Tyco. http://en.wikipedia.org/

Chapter 2

13   *Dawn of the Gods.* Jacquetta Hopkins Hawkes, Random House, NY:1968

27/28   *In Spite of the Gods: The Rise of Modern India.* Edward Luce. Qtd in "Drug Test", Ariel Levy. the New Yorker. Jan 2, 2012, p35

Chapter 3

29   *CIDA*, John Robert Colomba, Canadian Global almanac, MacMillan Canada; 1996.p205

29   Statistics Canada. Modified 2007-02-05. www.40.statscan.ca/101/cst/01/fami/112a.htm

29   BC Government Quick Facts Booklet, 1997.

30   *Health Care out of Control.* Bill Moyers, "NOW" PBS:May 17,2002. Quote by Dr. Dean Ornish

31   The cost of owning a Formula 1 car. http://www.tiscali.co.uk/sport/f1/f1parts.html

32   NBA salaries. http://www.usatoday.com/sports/nba/stories/2001-02-salaries.htm. April 16, 2002.

33   "The Selling of Free Trade." John R. McArthur. Hill & Wang, NY

34   *Arms Sales by Supplier Nations.* Richard F. Grimmett, CRS Report for Congress, Sept 26, 2007. Global Issues. August 25, 2008. www.globalissues.org/article/74/the-arms-trade-is-big-business.

35   General dynamics war contracts. Yahoo Finance quotes. May 30, 2002 http://ca.finance.yahoo.com/q?s=GD&d=c&t=2y&1=on&z=b&q=1

35   *Halliburton's work for army in Iraq* . . . Associated Press. Washington: May 30,2003

36-38   "Submarines, Secrets & Spies." *Nova*, PBS-TV: April 23, 2002

37   *Mysteries of the Deep.* Scientific American Frontiers TV series. PBS. Nov/Dec 2002

38   *Chief Seattle's letter.* Seattle WA, Archives: 1855

Chapter 4

42 *Brief appearance for Panghali.* The Delta Optimist, Delta, BC: March 24, 2007. P3

43 *En Garde.* Arthur Krystal, Book Review of "The Last Duel: A True Story of Death and Honor" by James Landale. New Yorker Magazine, NY: March 12, 2007

Chapter 5

47/48 *Why Men Don't Iron.* 3 part series. PBS TV. Quality Time TV Production. GB. 1998

54 *Complete Guide to Guys.* Dave Barry. Random House, NY: 1995 pp XIV & 57.

55 *B2Spirit.* Air force Link. http://www.af.mil/factsheets/factsheet/asp?fsID=82

55 *The Human Factor* . . . Kim Vicente. Taylor & Francis. NY:2004

Chapter 6

65 *The Chalice & the Blade.* Riane Eisler. Harper & Row, San Francisco: 1987

66 *Canadian Soldier Killed.* Graham Thomson. Canwest News Service. Vancouver Province: August 10,2008.

66 "No matter how you count, . . ." Stephen Hume. Vancouver Sun: January 19,2007 A9

66 Personal letter from Art Eggleton, Min of Defence, Govt of Canada, Ottawa: April 17,2002

69 *Americans Underestimate Iraqui Death Toll.* Nancy Benac. AP news. Feb 24,2007

69 Christopher Gelpi. www.duke.edu/~gelpi

70 *They can't see why they are hated.* Seamus Milne. The Guardian, London: Sept 12/2001

72 *Ramses the Great.* The Great Egyptians Series, The Learning Channel, TV: May 2002

72 *Battle of Kadesh.* Wikipedia online http://en.wikipedia.org/wiki/Battle_of_Qadesh

74 *Battle of Stalingrad.* http://en.wikipedia.org/wiki/Battle_of_Stalingrad

74/75 Land mine story—Senator Leahy http:/leahy.senate.gov/issues/landmines

78/79 "The Insufferable Gaucho." Roberto Bolano. Illiarionov quoted. New Yorker: Oct 1,2007. 76-77

79 China builds a massive warship base, Jonathan Manthorpe, Vancouver Sun, May 2, 2008. A11

Chapter 7
82 Health Care out of Control. Bill Moyers. "NOW" PBS:May17,2002.
Quote by Dr. Dean Ornish.
87 "Mexican Farmers demand protection from NAFTA" Mica Rosenberg/
Reuters. Vancouver Sun: Feb 1,2008
89 "The Economics of Empire" William Finnegan, Harper's Magazine. New
York: May 2003. 48-49
90 "Commanding Heights: The battle for the world economy." President of
Malaysia, quoted, PBS Detroit.
99 *Ain't I a Woman?* Sojourner Truth, convention in Ohio, 1851. Recorded
by Frances Gage.

Chapter 8
100 *Navigator: Passenger comforts.* Times-Colonist, Victoria. May 17,2002
C2
101 *Death by Traffic Accident*, 2005 Canadian Global almanac, John Wiley
& Sons, p58
Death by motor vehicle, American Almanac, 1996.

Chapter 9
108 *Media Ownership.* NOW. Bill Moyers, PBS TV April 26, 2002
111 Angry outbursts lead often to heart damage. Study by Dr. Murray
Mittleman of Harvard Medical School. Jamie Talan, Newsday. Times-
Colonist. Victoria: Sept 1,1995. C3
114 Dartmouth medical school study. Dr. James Sargent & Dr Madeline A.
Dalton, May 30,2002.

Chapter 10
117 *BC Pledges to streamline forestry code.* Judith Lavoie. Times-Colonist,
Victoria BC: May 2,2002. A1, A2
117/118 *Clayoquot Mass Trials.* Ronald McIsaac & Anne Champagne. New
Society Publishers: Jan 1995.
119 "Powder River Showdown" Opinion. New York Times. NY: Aug 4, 2002.
(online Aug28,2008)
120 "Can't lose weight . . ." Reuters News Service, NY. The Vancouver Sun,
Vancouver, May 15,2008 A15
124/125 *Buffalo Bill.* Wikipedia.
http://en.wikipedia.org/wiki/Buffalo_Bill August 28,2008
125 The Grass Which Grows . . . Rev John Beckewelder 1819. The Indian &
the White Man, ed. Wilcomb E. Washburn. Anchor Books: 1964

Chapter 11

128/129 *Dawn of the Gods*, Jacquetta Hopkins Hawkes, Random House NY:1968.

129 *The Chalice & the Blade*. Riane Eisler. Harper & Row, San Francisco: 1987. p30

129 *Goddess Remembered*, Donna Read, Director. National Film Board, Canada.

130 The Indian & the White Man, ed. Wilcomb Washburn. Anchor Books: 1964. John Lawson quotes, 47-49

132 Letter from Birmingham Jail, Martin Luther King Jr. April 16, 1963. Alabama.

135 Herman Golleb. Interview NOW, PBS TV: April 26, 2002.

Cecilia Tanner has written and published 5 books including Writing for Engineering, (McGraw Hill-Ryerson, 1993). She taught writing skills and English at the University of Victoria for 16 years to students in the business school, and in the arts, computer, and engineering faculties.

Ms. Tanner has a private pilot license, and has especially enjoyed tennis, skiing and kayaking for recreation. She is also an accomplished artist. She has lived on the West Coast of British Columbia, Canada, all her life.